Learn to Research

Tips for Scientific Working

Martin Gertler

Learn to Research

Tips for Scientific Working

learn2research.*net*

Bibliographic information of the German National Library:

The German National Library lists this publication in the German National Bibliography; detailed bibliographical data is available on the Internet at http://dnb.dnb.de

Production and Publisher: BoD – Books on Demand, Norderstedt

ISBN: 978-3-7481-5072-5

Preamble

All students need basic scientific skills and such basic knowledge is helpful to anyone who is involved in scientific studies and results, either privately or professionally.

A scientific paper is always a product that has its goal and should fulfil its purpose. This applies to every term paper at a university, as well as to presentations, project work and final theses. For this reason, learning to write scientific papers will be helpful in studies and professional practice, so that new knowledge can be created through research.

Science is when someone creates new knowledge scientifically!

Therefore, the principles and basics of scientific work cannot be reduced to the formalities of structuring and citation or to research and writing techniques, but rather to a consistently reearch attitude and approach: Whoever follows the approach of this book will no longer „write about something“, but want to investigate something – and this with the passion of a researcher.

The first German edition of this compilation of the basics of scientific research (2015) was published as a production of the Veganomics Institute to illustrate that even a scientific occupation with the vegan way of life always requires the respective scientific foundations and research results.

Furthermore, the principles of science also apply to other problems and solution goals of individuals and society, which is the reason why this book has been designed to be useful to everyone and to also serves as a companion book to our online course at the URL http://forschenlernen.jetzt (German) / http://learn2research.net (English) – it works as a transcription of all video lessons and follows them in its chapter structure and all headlines.

Berlin, October 2018

Martin Gertler

Table of contents

1 Science

What is science? It is easier to answer than the question, in which cases can be spoken of science at all, i.e. when science is approached scientifically and corresponding results are achieved.

Nevertheless, definitions should not be missing in this first chapter – they are indispensable too for scientific work.

Science should be understood in the context of this basic course as an activity of scientific work. Following Balzert et al.

- is science about an orderly approach with the aim of gaining new insights and knowledge as well as solving practical problems;
- concrete exploitation intentions are not a precondition for this;
- one ties to existing scientific knowledge and knows the current state of the art;
- its findings are published, which must be comprehensible and verifiable for others;
- scientific methods and recognized quality criteria are observed (cf. Balzert et al. 2011: 7 f.).

So when can we talk about science? Well, in any case – and here the brand is now set right at the beginning and with all emphasis – only *when someone creates new knowledge with science.*

To some ears, this may sound like a corny joke, but let us actually state this as a principle: only if we start – on the basis of existing knowledge and with the realization that what is available is not yet sufficient for the specific problem – with the aim of generating the new knowledge required in research, then we will work scientifically.

1.1   Findings as a Goal

Anyone who pursues science is therefore looking for a new insight that has been lacking so far. According to the German Science Council, research is a *„practice of its own kind, a practice of knowledge that first follows the logic of the search for truth"* (Wissenschaftsrat 2011: 11).

A scientist strives to obtain results that honestly answer his previously well-defined questions or help to solve problems that have previously been comprehensibly analysed, but he does not do so without first carefully checking what answers or solutions have already been offered to his question; and in any case he incorporates these existing knowledge stocks into his research. If these stocks are already sufficient for the knowledge objective, the research project will be regarded as unnecessary and abandoned.

Therefore it is always necessary to inform oneself at the beginning about the already given, current conditions of the science to the concrete question and to consider also possibly already existing opposing positions to the own solution idea.

The goal of knowledge in mind

This includes collecting information for every scientific project, as well as structuring and making operationalisable the already available data and knowledge. However, such a compilation alone is no longer considered sufficient for a research project, even if it is necessary in the course of a research project – a research project needs a beneficial knowledge goal.

Such an objective can lead to the formation of hypotheses, a theoretical sketch or the review of hypotheses or theories with a view to their applicability, thus preparing drafts or even concepts and strategies for their implementation through scientific procedures.

Disciplines

The fields of science can be distinguished by type and orientation:

- Formal and Structural Sciences – Mathematics and Computer Science
- Humanities – Philosophy, Theology and Cultural Studies
- Engineering – Civil Engineering, Electrical Engineering, Mechanical Engineering, etc.
- Natural Sciences – Biology, Chemistry and Physics
- Social sciences – comprise those fields of science that deal with the interrelationships of human coexistence and related actions and behaviours

For all of them, they are researching for the deepening and broadening of basic knowledge and for new findings for applicable solutions.

Although they have developed and apply clearly distinguishable methods, they share the fundamental approach of creating new knowledge on the basis of existing knowledge in a systematic, comprehensible and verifiable manner.

This distinguishes the disciplines of science from other solutions that we know from our everyday life – for example from intuition, from mere practical experience and from trial and error. Without previously proven knowledge that has been methodically and scientifically developed and tested, no one can set out on the path of scientific knowledge gain.

This also opens up the meaning of studying at a university. Those who only want to graduate in order to get a reasonably well paid job have not correctly set their own goal. Employers expect university graduates not only to know the customs of their scientific discipline, but even to be able to apply them, which means systematically generating the new knowledge that is needed in the practical environment of the company in a scientifically manner, i.e. methodically and taking existing knowledge into account.

This applies fundamentally, but also at every moment: When a professional question and challenge comes up, university graduates proceed scientifically – not purely intuitively, relying on practical experience or simply trying it out.

Therefore, this basic knowledge for conduct scientific working is indispensable and important for all of them.

1.2 Doing Research

On April 1, 2015, someone at „gutefrage.net" wanted to know: *„When will scientific work be used?"* In reply, there appeared briefly and just within a few minutes this: *„It will be used in research"* (cf. KoraChany 2015).

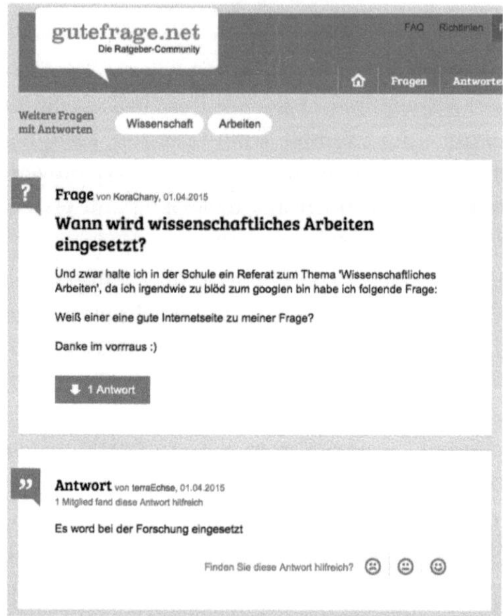

Figure 1: Question and Answer at gutefrage.net

(Source: Screenshot of a question by KoraChany 2015)

The reverse conclusion to this correct answer is: If *scientific work is to be carried out, research is necessary*, so it cannot be a mere essay.

In this respect, scientific work should be defined as research work, so that the practice to be found at some universities is also contradicted, scientific work may *„be produced according to scientific quality criteria, but cannot make a substantial contribution to research"* (Balzert et al. 2011: 54).

However, the authors themselves ruled out this possibility a short time later by stating that a question should not be dealt with as part of a scientific work without relevance for their own scientific discipline (cf. Balzert et al. 2011: 63; cf. also the scientific quality criterion „relevance" there: 32 ff.).

The Science Council also underlines that good research is distinguished by relevance (cf. Science Council 2011: 11), whereby relevance is only mentioned in science if a research contribution is actually created.

From many years of practical experience at universities it can be concluded that every scientific work always requires a clear *problem, objective and research question* in order to be able to achieve a result, otherwise no scientific work arises.

Here, scientificity is thus not understood as reduced to formal matters – such as structure, citations, directories etc. And since every researcher is required to bring in the existing findings of his own field of science, he adds his new knowledge there and thus makes a research contribution, however high or low this may be assessed by others.

1.3   Method-guided Results

The former director of the Max Planck Institute in Munich, Hans-Peter Dürr, made it clear in an exciting interview about his approach and results, how just someones own approach determines his results.

Figure 2: Interview with Hans-Peter Dürr

(Source: Screenshot from Gertler 1997b)

Dürr said in his statement that he wanted to indicate that the reality of the natural scientist is one that appears to him as such, but that it is not the actual reality of nature.

He used the parable of a fisherman who had come to two „basic laws of fishing" on the basis of his personal experience of years of fishing: firstly, all fish were larger than five centimetres, and secondly, all fish had gills.

The fisherman simply calls both of these basic laws, since these facts have proved so true with every catch that he can assume that this will always be the case in the future.

Then the fisherman met with the philosopher, who told him that the five-centimeter statement was certainly not a fundamental law: the mesh size of the net had rather determined that smaller fish could not be caught. But the fisherman was not impressed, because what he could not catch with his net was simply not fish for him.

He, Hans-Peter Dürr, transfers this image to the natural sciences, which again and again claimed that they had found something and that what they found was a characteristic of nature – and not rather a characteristic that nature reveals to them through their measuring methods and so on. (cf. Hans-Peter Dürr in Gertler 1997b from 22:30 until 24:22)

In this case, it was the mesh size of the net that determined what could be caught and thus declared and examined as fish. The method of measurement and its possibilities have noticeable consequences for the result, and to a significant degree – the parable made this clear.

More generally, we always examine with criteria measuring and judging that actually predetermine our results; what we have not measured or analyzed is not available to us as a result – and it may be precisely these results, often data, that we need to explain or solve a problem.

And another thing: on the basis of the data we have obtained, we are quickly tempted to make general statements, and then the laws of logic such as: Since this is – as is perhaps often the case – a fundamental problem on which we now have data and could come up with a solution, we could draw one or two general conclusions from it.

Can we really? No. Scepticism is the order of the day – and this is exactly what Hans-Peter Dürr encouraged us to do, because his fisherman had invented that universally valid „basic law of fishing", according to which fish are always at least five centimeters long simply because of the mesh size of his net, whereas the fisherman's neighbour and competitor might throw out a net whose mesh is eight centimeters long; his „basic law" would then mean that fish are always at least eight centimeters long? (Reading tip: Dürr 2011)

Interdisciplinary Work

When the scientist Hans-Peter Dürr has the history of the fishing net and its meshes in mind, he is as a physicist at work, measuring and determining his result based on the data – right down to the natural law.

Other sciences have different approaches: in the humanities, for example, logic, plausibility and understanding are among the necessary tools of the scientist's trade; in the social sciences, for example, contextual knowledge is gained and deepened statistically and empirically.

And if the methods of their own discipline are sometimes not sufficient for them, scientists also go beyond their own borders and conduct interdisciplinary research; in the course of their project they then incorporate phases in which they make useful use of instruments from other disciplines. For example, empirical methods of social science are often also used by other disciplines to support the formation of hypotheses or theories or to test the suitability and validity of a thesis for everyday use. (Reading tip: Jungert 2010)

1.4   The Truth of the Results

Earlier, Hans-Peter Dürr had already made clear in his parable of the fishing net what paradigm the sciences determine: they search for truth and all too willingly want to make binding statements about it – which is not only in the nature of the researcher, but often also results from the expectations of his clients.

It suggests that we take a closer look at this claim – and do so in a thoroughly critical manner.

We will talk to the psychotherapist and constructivist Paul Watzlawick about the theoretical demands that Sir Karl Raimund Popper has given us on the path of scientific work and we will encounter other paradigms of science with which we must be familiar.

Outdated Views

Paul Watzlawick in an interview at his former workplace at the Mental Research Institute in Palo Alto, California in 1997, had already pointed out that in his subject, psychotherapy, it is still assumed that there is a „real reality“ which the so-called mentally normal and thus above all the therapists are aware of, whereas the so-called mentally ill people have a distorted view of this reality.

This view has long been abolished in other branches of science and is simply no longer tenable, he said.

Figure 3: Interview with Paul Watzlawick

(Source: Screenshot from Gertler 1997c)

In today's epistemology, it is the task of science to develop procedures that are effective for a very specific purpose:*"This may very well mean that in five years' time this current, best way of dealing with the problem will already be replaced by a better way"* (Watzlawick in Gertler 1997c).

This epistemological view also suggests not wanting to achieve general and timelessly valid findings, but to concentrate on the concrete and current purpose of the solution of a possibly even locally limited existing problem of knowledge and to really limit oneself to it.

If we want to follow Paul Watzlawick's view and get involved in possible questions of veganomics for example, thus the vegan economy in the narrower and broader sense, we'll no longer ask: *How can farmers grow bio-vegan in order to achieve economic returns and not go bankrupt?* or: *What is the difference between managing a vegan and a conventional supermarket?*

We must get away from general attempts to respond, because in fact they are as good as never possible and true – we must instead focus on attempts to solve very specific and limited challenges.

Doesn't scientific work then always stick to detail? What can I learn from it and take with me if I am allowed only to repeatedly find out the factors and criteria for individually valid results?

The answer to this may be: We do not learn any solution steps that can always be repeated in terms of content, when working scientifically, but we learn the procedures for identifying possible solutions per se.

For organic vegans farmers who have to survive economically over a long period of time, we do not provide panaceas, but rather have to find out in depth the determining factors of their specific problem in order to be able to find a suitable solution for them.

And the prospective manager of a vegan supermarket is not helped by a basic manager's manual, but only by the ability to analyse the competitive situation, the sources of supply, the target groups and their presence in a defined area, and so on – and all that has to be trained in scientific practice.

Paul Watzlawick has given us the idea that it is the task of science to develop procedures that are effective for a specific purpose; the more and the more often we ourselves develop such procedures as solutions, the better we will be trained in developing scientific solutions.

This is precisely why we always need our own practice of scientific work, as it is realized in the university environment through appropriate assignments in homework, project work and final theses.

1.5   Falsification as a Working Principle

Sir Karl Raimund Popper has made significant contributions to epistemological and scientific theory, criticising a common notion of science according to which conclusions for scientific theories are generalised on the basis of concrete observations.

Let us take as an example the everyday „knowledge" or rather the everyday idea that we humans „by nature" are dependent on food of animal origin, as we had mostly grown up, programmed with slogans like „meat is a piece of vitality" and „milk makes tired men lively", as a result of which many contemporaries have the immovable belief that without such food it would not be possible to survive, otherwise we would soon become ill and die prematurely.

The majority of physicians and nutritionists still adhere to this idea of a necessary nutrition with animal components, all of whom had once enjoyed their scientific training and were influenced there by the scientific state of knowledge at that time, which described the so called mixed diet as healthy and necessary.

The mantra of a healthy mixed diet therefore also lives from scientific results, even if today's state of knowledge makes this thinking obsolete.

Whereas we had just learned from Paul Watzlawick that much knowledge has become obsolete after some time through new findings and investigations, we now learn from Karl Popper another critical view on the handling of scientifically based theories. Decades ago he rejected all inductively written theories (based on observations) as uncertain speculations and demanded that they should be overturned by searching for conflicting observations.

This becomes quite easy to understand with the example of the claim that all swans are white. Such an assertion can only last until the first black swan is seen, and when the first black swan appeared, the previous theory of the always white swans became of course immediately „falsified", i.e. recognized as false and rejected.

Back to our previously chosen example – to the claim that people need food of animal origin: This claim, called knowledge, is currently already being refuted in more than a million cases in Germany every day – because 1.5 percent of people in Germany were already living vegan in 2015, i.e. without food of animal origin or ingredients (cf. veganomics.de 2014).

The theory of the necessity of a diet with animal components, supported by a lot of funding and research, has thus long since been falsified by the everyday life, observable to everyone.

However, this does not mean that the majority of people would immediately reject such a clearly outdated and refuted theory as that of the necessity of animal food components – on the contrary, we experience in many areas of our daily lives that earlier theories seem to be wrong: in the areas of economy, ecology, politics, health, but still many people sometimes cling very vigorously to outdated and refuted ideas and theories.

From Sir Karl Raimund Popper we take with us a fundamentally critical attitude: Always examine what is being claimed – and even be motivated to search for anything that could contradict this assertion – simply so that merely claimed, observation-supported facts do not become allegedly „valid" theories that no one can contradict any more – simply so that false „truths" do not remain – with reference to their, in earlier times, still possible – but provisional – confirmation.

In addition, Popper points out, that nothing can be „verified" that is, declared *true* forever and ever, because we cannot rule out any situation for now and for the future that contradicts the theory previously written.

As long as we have not (yet) succeeded in falsifying an assertion or even theory, according to Popper it is by no means considered verified, but always only „provisionally confirmed", and the result „verified" can therefore and logically never exist.

> The assumption that a diet which is necessary to maintain our health with animal ingredients has not been „provisionally confirmed" for decades, to sum up Sir Popper's approach, but has long since been refuted, „falsified"; it is therefore not true; such claims are clearly wrong according to today's knowledge.

Why is this important for all of us? Because since Popper it has been one of the natural tasks of every scientist not to continue to use disproved claims and theories – and once is really enough – but to reject them. To identify and consider these refutations is one of the principles of our scientific work.

Thus, after Watzlawick, also Popper should have made clear once again how important a consistent practice of scientific work is for us: It protects us from considering „commonplaces" to be true and correct, and it motivates us to search for investigations that have examined the alleged with the goal of falsification.

This prevents us from creating unsuitable solutions with invalid theories. (Reading tip: Popper 1966)

1.6   Science and Communication

At this point, hermeneutics – another important term that deals with the basics and processes of understanding – is not only typical for and in the possession of humanities scholars; let's remember Hans–Peter Dürr or take Paul Watzlawick's statements: Understanding statements and contexts, but also one's own methodology and approach, is indispensable in order to be able to be scientifically active at all, which sounds banal, but it has a significant fundamental component.

Understanding requires dealing with the possibilities of understanding of others. Anyone who works scientifically must be able to understand and interpret sources and statements and data and make them usable for his knowledge goal, and he must be able to make his own paths and findings comprehensible to others.

Understanding is trained in interpersonal dialogues and in dealing with statements and texts from areas of everyday life and culture, other than one's own. (Reading tip: Jung 2012)

Science requires Dialogue

A scientist always works with existing literature and often in exchange with other researchers, even from other disciplines. In addition, universities and other research institutions usually have mentoring relationships or concrete cooperation phases with other researchers.

The researcher enters into a dialogue with others at the latest when the results are published, often even in the case of interim results, and there is feedback and correction advice, which is why it is necessary to be prepared for this technical communication from the outset and to design everything written in such a way that it is easily comprehensible and verifiable for others.

With such a dialogic attitude, a researcher ensures that he can not only develop a solution that is useful in the defined context for his own purposes, but that he also makes his approach and results, including method applications, transparent and thus useful to all others.

Research and Development

This benefit from new knowledge gained through research is often used as a basis for application in development, and new research topics can also arise from development (cf. Balzert et al. 2011: 49 f.).

In this respect, the „R&D"-areas – typically found in companies – often refer to the interaction between applied research and development activities.

And yet it is precisely the relativity of „R&D" that must always remain in view: the insights gained are valid for a certain time or period and for a certain context – mostly nothing more, see Paul Watzlawick. And they are to be rejected if they have not withstood a falsifying inspection, even in one single case – see Sir Karl Raimund Popper.

1.7   Reality Constructions

Findings that have been developed into theories can very soon be outdated or have simply been disproved – although they often have a formative effect on our reality and in other cases hardly at all.

- It's become clear that the consumption of meat products promotes or even triggers so-called diseases of civilization; it is also clear that it is responsible for life-threatening antibiotic resistance, which in Germany causes up to 40,000 deaths each year, according to research by journalists (cf. ZEIT ONLINE 2014) – but meat consumption is not declining noticeably.

- It has long been clear that Apple will soon introduce a new iPhone „generation" – and it is also expected that many people will again do everything they can do to get one of the very first devices of this kind into their possession, even though they do not really need it and even though its production unnecessarily pollutes and exploits our environment, people, animals and resources.

In both cases, such information could lead to a conclusion like this: „Attention, harmfully" – but logical conclusions cannot be expected because of this information, so there is obviously no „mechanical" connection between the knowledge gained and any resulting action.

The question arises as to the reality of our reality – or rather: our realities. In recent decades, cognitive theorists have described „constructivism" as a paradigm, a frame of reference that is important for our scientific work. Finally, we investigate realities: through analysis, questioning, interpretation and understanding of sources of different kinds. But how can we ensure that we have grasped them „correctly" and can thus arrive at valid results?

The basic idea of constructivism is that man does not passively receive in the perception of his fellow world, but that he builds up his own world by selection, projection and assignment of meaning from what his senses provide (cf. Pörksen 2002). He „constructs" his world in an individual matter, but this is shaped by social and cultural conditions too.

Man as a self-designing, self-contained system always knows only something about himself, but never something about the reality outside himself. Although the „radical constructivists" do not deny the existence of this reality, they fundamentally deny man the possibility of experiencing something about it and of knowing how the real reality is constituted.

If we can only develop notions of reality according to the state of knowledge and the operating method of our brains, but cannot directly access something like „reality" (cf. Weischenberg 1998: 60), we have to think about subjective realities. Standards oriented towards absoluteness such as „true" or „right" will then give way to the yardstick of viability: what is or was „useful", „helpful", „successful" in that situation and according to the respective point of view.

This constructivism initially seems to us to be incompatible with our traditional, ontologically oriented thinking, which always assumes that something is like this and not different.

Even a sentence like „These are facts" suggests the irrefutable, the given, the present – in accordance with our longing for the definitive, whereby a closer look at the word „factum" proves to be an indication of something completely different: „made" would be the literal translation of the Latin word „factum", just as the word „facts" reveals that things have obviously been done by someone.

Radical constructivism is a theory of cognition, in which cognition no longer concerns an „objective" reality, but the order and organization of experiences. The real difference between constructivism and ontological thinking lies in the assessment of the relationship between knowledge and reality. Man can only know how he came to his idea of reality, but he cannot therefore say something definitive about „the reality" outside of himself: Only his own failure says something about this „reality". If someone gets angry, stumbles, gets stranded – he knows that his idea of reality did not fit.

Science speaks in a similar way that a hypothesis can only be falsified, but not verified, because conditions could arise at any time that refute a preliminary confirmation. Apparently there is no definitive truth available for us.

For the constructivist, knowledge is not knowledge of reality outside of himself, but only the consciousness of the operations of the brain, the result of which is our world of experience. This insight is important to him.

1.8   Suitable Procedures

Science responsibly concentrates on raising awareness of the operations that have led to a result: traceability, transparency and verifiability are quality criteria that have to do with this.

In our everyday scientific work, we rely above all on the tried and tested – i.e. on what has allegedly proven itself through repetition and has not yet been refuted. (Reading tip: Von Foerster 1997)

Figure 4: Interview with Siegfried Peterseim

(Source: Screenshot from Gertler 1997a)

Astronomer Siegfried Peterseim for example explained that in the case of the stars, the distance to Earth can be measured by using the orbit of the Earth around the Sun. The further away the star is from us, the smaller the displacement of the star is. In the case of the galaxies further away, the greater the shift of light to the red end of the spectrum; the further away the star system is from us, the greater it is. (Cf. Peterseim in Gertler 1997a from 0:01:38)

As long as this method of measurement has not yet been replaced or refuted by a more precise one, it will continue to apply. It is viable and can be used scientifically for as long as it lasts – and that means that we remain aware of its conditionality and approach in accordance with constructivist epistemology.

Is there really no immovable reality? You will say: yes, it's there, because of the laws of nature! No, would I say: „laws of nature" as a concept created by man for something very static, God-given, should therefore be problematic.

I am presenting you Hans-Peter Dürr, an astrophysicist who had his well considered reservations and explained them:

„Nor do the laws of nature apply in the way we believe they do, in the old mechanistic form that something runs like a clockwork, but the laws of nature are also just a result of evolution, that they have evolved, probably also so that other possibilities of legal arrangement were possible, but it is so locked in a certain way, almost like a habit. I always remember when I'm driving in the train and it starts to rain and I see the water running down the window – so you have to be careful how the water tries to get down. It comes down in the most crooked ways, but once it has found a path, all the water goes that way. And then I come and ask: Why did the water go exactly

this path? There could have been another path, but once it has found its way, it be-comes a kind of natural law for right now for the run-off of water. That's how the laws came into being." (Hans-Peter Dürr, in Gertler 1997b at 5:16)

Hans-Peter Dürr referred to the constructivist's „fitting", without saying it directly: rainwater chose a way down on the pane – or paved it for itself; the way did not have to be exactly this one way, but it only had to fit at that moment, today and only on this one window pane, for the drainage of water.

In scientific work, we focus on „appropriate" procedures to achieve usable results – whether they really are the „appropriate" procedures, but only become evident after the fact. Of course, we observe the guidelines of the methods we choose, which were not created by God as immovable natural laws in the act of creation of the world, but by testing them in constant application, solely aimed at fitting according to the scientific quality criteria for the achievement of results.

This also ensures objectivity – after all, constructivist thinking does not stand for the justification of arbitrariness, but rather asks about the conditions under which a point of view or insight comes about. We ensure objectivity in scientific work through objective presentation, a representative selection of arguments and counter-arguments, a clear description, correct interpretation and the consideration of objections.

1.9 Task Sheet for this Chapter

Support your self-study through these tasks!

1. What are the main features of the concept of science?

2. How do the fields of science differ – and what do they have in common?

3. Describe the interdisciplinary approach using a conceivable example, such as your own project.

4. Why do the sciences, according to Hans-Peter Dürr, not discover properties of nature – and what is your view on his view that the methods used predetermine the result?

5. How do you understand Paul Watzlawick's criticism of the idea of a „real reality" – and what does it mean for your own idea: reinforcement or questioning? What consequences do you draw from this for your own project?

6. If we don't want to develop general answers, but rather learn how to identify possible solutions: Which ones are already known or even familiar to you?

7. What consequences for your own first or next investigation could Sir Karl R. Popper's call have for conflicting observations to be sought in order to refute theories and claims?

8. Discuss – with a view to a question to be explored by yourself – the constructivist view, according to which knowledge cannot refer to reality outside of man, but only to the consciousness of the operations of one's own thinking and procedure.

2 Quality Criteria

There is no complete and definitive set of quality criteria for scientific work that would have been adopted as binding by an appropriate body.

Nevertheless, generally accepted criteria of principle and criteria of importance for empirical work can be defined.

Fundamental criteria:

1 Purposefulness
2 Distinctiveness
3 Relevance
4 Logic
5 Traceability
6 Honesty
7 Verifiability
8 Transparency

Criteria for Empirical Work:

9 Validity
10 Reliability
11 Significance
12 Representativeness

Fundamental Criteria

The following quality criteria of scientific excellence apply to all types of scientific work – i.e. in everyday university life, which in the event of success in Germany always ends with a scientific degree – for homework, papers, projects and theses.

2.1 Purposefulness

Science has only one goal: to create new knowledge through research. This orientation must be recognizable as a leitmotif in a scientific work, so that you do not write „about a topic", you do not „choose" a topic – but you'll look for an object of research that can be worked on within the framework of the guidelines.

When students begin to tell me: „I would like to write about..." – then I interrupt them and explain that the point is not to write an essay about something, but to examine something with clear objectives and a clean methodical approach in order to achieve a result and thus create new knowledge.

Science is *a goal-oriented but open-ended activity* It is impossible to predict whether and how the expected or desired result will be achieved.

The goal of „writing about something" is not one that could be scientific – neither could the goal of „conceiving something", i.e. achieving a practical goal, be suitable for a scientific work.

Focusing exclusively on one specific research objective is therefore a first, indispensable and fundamental quality criterion for scientific excellence.

2.2   Distinctiveness

If research means gaining new knowledge on the basis of what has already been researched and with the help of new arguments, results etc. and by following a comprehensible path and using suitable and proven methods, it can be concluded that each scientific work is and must be unique. For this reason no research topics that have already been carried out by someone else in a comparable manner are allowed to be dealt with at universities.

However, the distinctiveness may not only lie in the choice of topic, i.e. in the problem and objective – it may also be justified in the choice of method.

As an example of the criterion distinctiveness through interdisciplinary method selection may serve my own humanities investigation, the results of which were examined with a quantitative content analysis of audience feedback by letters (cf. the conceptual model at Gertler 1999: 169). Here an empirical method frequently used in communication science – the quantitative content analysis – was chosen to use a sample of audience letters to examine a previously purely humanities thesis. This interdisciplinary approach using the multiple regression analysis was a new and special feature for the humanities discipline in which the research project was located.

2.3   Relevance

A recognisable orientation towards the specificity of one's own scientific question or approach can also create the relevance that makes the work that arises as a result of research significant for the associated scientific discipline.

After all, research has to bring new findings, that is its relevance, and this claim therefore applies to any scientific task, whatever its scope.

Relevance as a quality criterion of scientific excellence therefore refers primarily to the significance for one's own scientific field, but not to the significance for the field of application in professional practice, for which research may be carried out in a specific case.

Relevant for scientific work is what contributes to scientific progress and creates new knowledge in one's own field of expertise.

2.4   Logic

Scientific work does not claim any result, but reveals the complete development of this result. All assumptions, arguments and conclusions must be explicitly derived, logically justified and critically discussed.

Each chain of argumentation must be clearly and structurally presented, from the premises to the conclusion.

*   The *inductive* logic starts from individual observations and concludes that what is behind the observed could be a general pattern („If X and Y present themselves in this way, then Z is likely to...“). Inductive arguments conclude from individual observations on the whole – the conclusion is therefore only true with a certain probability.

*   The *deductive* logic concludes that in these or those conditions the result must look like this or that („If X has these values and Y has those values, then it must apply to Z that...“) The conclusions of deductive reasoning are true in any case if the premises and reasons are true.

It is important to be careful to reflect and justify the logic of one's own arguments and conclusions over and over again – even every reader not involved in the investigation must be able to understand that and why every logical connection claimed in the work actually exists.

2.5   Traceability

The entire research process is affected by it, as are all contents of the resulting publication.

If third parties cannot understand why and how a research project was structured, where the problem was located, which goal was set, which sources and data were used and for which reasons, or if the principles of logical reasoning were not adhered to – then there you can't talk abaout scientific work.

Balzert et al. make it clear that the content and procedure in scientific works must be accessible to the reader or listener and explicitly place the criterion of traceability in connection with other quality criteria, which are discussed separately there: with objectivity, verifiability, reliability, validity, comprehensibility, relevance and logical reasoning (vgl. Balzert u. a. 2011: 43 ff.). This makes clear the fundamental importance attached to the quality criterion of traceability.

2.6   Honesty

The plagiarism cases that have become public in recent years in research work have contributed to honesty becoming known as a fundamental quality criterion on which much depends:

> *„Honesty towards oneself and others is first and foremost, and is both the ethical norm and the basis for the rules of scientific professionalism, i.e. good scientific practice, which vary from discipline to discipline, and one of the core tasks of universities"* (cf. Deutsche Forschungsgemeinschafti 1998: 5).

Honesty in dealing with sources as well as with external and own results does not rule out any errors, but effectively helps to avoid them. Therefore, the criterion of honesty requires that all data, analyses and statements adopted or produced be checked before they are included in the solution.

Honesty creates credibility and also refers to the way in which texts and design are presented, which should always be objective and neutral in scientific work.

A claiming or tendentious style of writing would be a violation of honesty simply because it would obscure sources or support or discriminate against positions, whereas the scientific – i.e. purely argumentative, questioning and concluding – style of writing ensures an honest and objectively oriented approach. This also requires consistent resistance to the temptation to embellish one's own scientific product not only in text but also optically and creatively.

It would also be dishonest not to conduct research in a work that merely looks scientific in form, but to conceive or design something practical, because in these cases we work towards a desired, i.e. a given result, for example by creating a marketing concept for a company or designing a product of whatever kind.

Those who conduct honest research also treat others fairly and assume their responsibility and role as researchers towards fellow researchers, supervisors and their own scientific discipline.

2.7   Verifiability

This criterion sounds trivial, but it is not if we bear in mind that every conclusion, every assumption, every hypothesis must be formulated in such a way that it can be verified.

This means that all formulations contain terms and conditions of such a nature that are sufficiently clear for third parties to come to the same or comparable conclusions.

Every hypothesis must be formulated in such a way that it can be verified – with Popper's goal of falsification.

In addition, all used sources must be verifiable and controllable, used quotations must be comparable to and correspond to the original.

This means that all sources that are not published – i.e. all regular university theses below a doctoral thesis and also all study books and materials, such as those used in distance learning courses – cannot be used because what cannot be verified by third parties who only have public access to sources cannot be cited, since not everyone can verify it.

Contributing to verifiability is to formulate key statements such as assumptions or hypotheses that can be refuted, to document and justify one's own approach and to clearly present the intermediate and final results.

It is necessary to describe the measuring instruments, tools and methods used and to disclose the origin of the data used.

In addition, graphics and illustrations, appendices and tables help to understand the process from the question to finding a solution.

In the case of Internet sources, the URL and the date of retrieval must also be specified in the list of sources (i.e. not in the footnotes or in text references).

2.8   Transparency

In principle, it must be clear whether and to what extent results can be investigated openly and thus independently in this work – this is a critical but important point, especially in contract research: scientific rather than practice-oriented objectives serve to ensure the scientific character of the project. Any clients and partners of the project must be named and their interests or specifications or influences described.

For example, if you are looking for a survey to help you market and sell a new vegan product, you need to identify the client's interest and objective, which means that your work can be better tested for relevance and value by remaining with this example.

Empirical Criteria

For empirical research further quality criteria are important, which will be presented here in an overview. In such a basic course, the peculiarities of empirical research – namely the utilization of experiences, opinions and points of view or also the behaviour of people – can only be touched upon, therefore the following quality criteria of empirical research may not be considered complete, but only fundamental.

2.9   Validity

It records the accuracy with which something is tested. Thus, measurements that do not fulfil the measurement purpose are not valid, even those that are too small samples that are not representative and incorrectly selected samples lead to inapplicable results.

So what is a sample? If, for example, you want to interview three hundred people online or through personal interviewers about their eating habits, then these three hundred cases are your „sample".

Why you want to question these three hundred people and which characteristics they should fulfil (e.g.: eat vegan / this for at least three years / live in Germany), you have to determine in your research design.

The definition of a sample includes the determination of the population for which you have selected this sample. Since the three characteristics mentioned above suggest that you want to find out something about many more people than just the concrete respondents – so you now also have to define your population precisely.

Suppose you want to find out something about a population that has the three characteristics of the sample just described, but you also want to be able to say something about people between the ages of 20 and 30 – then this criterion belongs to determining your sample and thus to conducting your survey and evaluating it, otherwise it is not valid.

Validity also affects the substantive argumentation of a scientific assignment. For example, logical errors can lead to a loss of the validity of the entire project. Typical sources of error are search questions with too much scope for answers, too small samples and incorrectly selected samples that are not representative of the population.

2.10 Reliability

This is the measurement accuracy, which in the ideal case is so good that if the measurement is repeated under constant conditions, the same results are again achieved.

To stick to the example just outlined: If your questionnaire is available and also precise instructions on the selection criteria under which candidates may be interviewed at all, then this should basically ensure that a new survey will at least rightly lead to similar and not to completely different results.

In the case of non-empirical work, reliability affects the requirement that an investigation based on the available materials can come to the same results.

2.11 Significance

Significance here means that an above random correlation can be assumed, whereby a threshold has previously been defined for the randomness.

Significance checks must be carried out in order to determine or exclude possible random influences based on mathematical probability calculation, taking into account the relationship between the selected sample sizes and the results of the significance calculations.

With the selected example thus for instance for correlations between a vegan lifestyle and age and place of residence could be searched. However, in the case of only three hundred respondents it is hardly to be expected that the variable place of residence could lead to significant results – the sample would probably be too small for this (cf. on the connection between the terms characteristic and variable Hennecke et al. 2001).

However, a significant correlation between „vegan" and „age" might be conceivable; this depends, however, on the more precise question that led to the establishment of the variables.

The criterion of significance already makes it clear that empirical research requires a great deal of expertise and arguments that are always logically comprehensible.

2.12　Representativity

In the social sciences, representativeness of quantitative results is important; therefore, a sample is defined in relation to a population and, as a rule, significantly higher case numbers are required for the investigation than for the qualitative approach.

Our case study has already shown that the more differentiated the variables are, the greater the number of cases required, and that certain standards must be observed in representative surveys, especially if, for example, a result is to be achieved for „the Germans“: although television ratings are only calculated for a few thousand households, these households have been carefully selected so that they actually „represent“ the inhabitants of this country and thus ensure their representativeness.

2.13　Task Sheet for this Chapter

Support your self–study through these tasks!

1. Which of the quality criteria mentioned are particularly noteworthy for you – with a view to a question that concerns you and is to be researched – for what reasons?

2. What could be the distinctiveness of your own project and how could it be helpful?

3. How could you formally fulfil the criterion of logical reasoning in your project? Confront this claim with your practice in the formulation of headings, the structuring, the setting of paragraphs, etc.

4. What consequences do you draw from the criterion of honesty for your writing style, your way of citation and the references (reference management)?

5. How can you investigate in an open manner – do targets or other influences exist and to what extent can you make them transparent?

6. Which of the empirical criteria could apply to you – and how will you try to meet them?

3 Researching

Research processes are basically always similar:

1. A *problem* is defined – it can be recognized by the user or specified as an order.

2. A suitable *specific research objective* must be formulated and justified. Without a goal there is no way! The goal to be defined must have a comprehensible reason, a context of discovery (including the defined problem) and a context of reasoning and analysis. Sometimes a larger and broader goal appears more luring than a smaller goal limited to clearer events, but is it a characteristic of scientificity to limit itself to what can be explored in the given time and with the possibilities given at all. Moreover, goals that are too broad cannot usually be met, since more variables and factors could play a role than one would be able to take into account.

3. A *research question* must be developed that also refers to the method to be chosen. The research question must be developed in conjunction with the objective. If it is difficult to formulate the research question in a redeemable way, then the objective must be critically reviewed again: Is it too broad, too open, too inaccurate?

4. The *research method* must be explained and its use justified. The choice of methods to be used does not follow personal preferences, but rather the objective and research question. If empirical methods are to be used, they must be chosen according to the method(s) of research and you must indicate why and with what (sub)objective they are to be used.

5. The *procedure* and its phases must be determined and planned, so the research plan must now be drawn up, taking into account all the above key points and putting them in a meaningful order, as well as providing starting points for financing options, cooperation, reviews and, if necessary, for partial publications in journals and papers for congresses.

6. The defined phases must be *carried out*, if necessary interim reports are required. The implementation follows the previous planning, but will always be open to unexpected changes due to interim results or external influences. It is important to keep a good record of your own procedure and all events that have influenced it – especially if third-party funds (external financing) are involved.

7. The *results* obtained are to be evaluated, critically discussed and presented. The final phase of the research project aims at a comprehensible and orderly presentation of all achieved results, including negative results. It is not decisive whether a result is „successful" with regard to a hoped-for goal, but it is decisive whether it came about and was presented in a scientifically honest and comprehensible manner.

The research project does not end with the review by the reviewers and/or with the publication, but is made available to third parties for their further research. It is possible that these third parties will confirm the results, possibly even refute them – this external validation is important, it is in principle open to results, and what actually happens in this phase following the research project should be approached with excitement and gratitude by the former researcher.

3.1   Types of Research

The quality criterion of purposefulness had already pointed out that research is not about the conception but about the investigation of something, which now needs to be deepened, as well as the question of whether the inductive or the deductive approach should be chosen – and what these two terms mean here.

We distinguish between explorative, constructive and empirical research.

- Exploratory investigations track down new problems, structure the findings, i.e. they explore the area under investigation and thus prepare the ground for further investigations, thus having an important function in science.

- Constructive research seeks scientific solutions for solving a previously identified and defined problem; this is a frequently occurring orientation in everyday university life for our students.

- Finally, empirical research examines the feasibility or applicability of a model, hypothesis or solution assumption, and it does this with proven and described methods, often through the quantitative use of data, but sometimes also through the qualitative use of statements.

Examples:

- Determining the CO_2 balance of food with the help of data from the Federal Ministry for the Environment is an explorative approach (cf. Hagen 2014).

- An investigation of chances and risks for an investment in the establishment of a company for vegan education realizes constructive research.

- The international research project „Communication Messages and Personal Diet Choices" of our institute deals with the question of how media communication and personal communication interact in the choice of diet and lifestyle; this can only be done with the help of self-developed hypotheses and their examination by means of surveys, so empirical research is carried out here.

It should be noted that empirical methods can be part of exploratory and constructive approaches.

3.2   Research and practice

Anyone who pursues science is looking for a new insight that he has not yet gained. Therefore, science is *a goal-oriented but open-ended activity* and it is impossible to predict whether the expected or desired result will actually be achieved.

However, university work often aims at a practical goal, not a research goal. For example, a business plan should be drawn up, a campaign designed or even a concept developed.

This way would not a new insight, but a kind of product – such as an instruction manual or a measure – defined as a goal.

In this respect, the practice to be found in some places is contradicted here that scientific work must be prepared according to scientific quality criteria, but does not itself need to make a substantial contribution to research.

Science must always act with an open mind. This is not even possible with pre-defined practical goals, where a concept or even a functioning product has to be achieved at the end, and often according to external specifications.

A Practicable Way

The *scientific* character can be ensured, however, if one *does not* set *the actual conception or design* as an objective. Instead, the scientific examination of the means and recipes desired or conceivable for such a conception or design will be defined as the objective of the study.

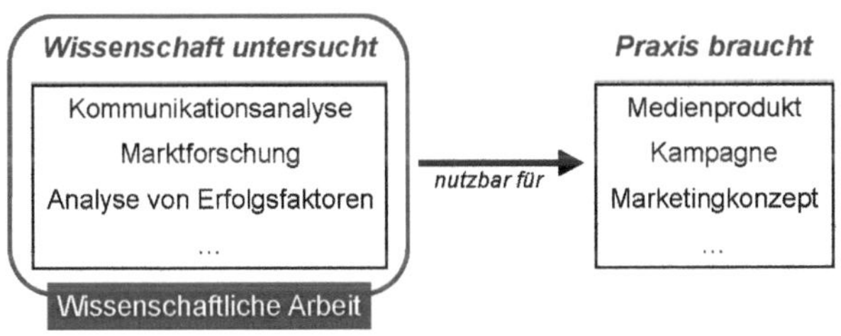

Unterschiedliche Zielsetzungen

Figure 5: Objectives of Science and Practice

(Source: own presentation)

Translation of Figure 5:

Science is investigating:	usable for:	**Practice needs:**
Communication analysis		Media product
Market research		Campaign
Analysis of success factors		Marketing plan
...		...

[Scientific work]

Different Objectives

This leaves the researcher the *Freedom of Science*: he may then come to the conclusion that some of the means and formulations perhaps preferred by practitioners are of little use for the specific application.

A scientific paper will therefore not always deliver a „positive" result in the eyes of the practitioners – namely what they had hoped for.

From a scientific point of view, any scientific result that has been achieved „cleanly" from a methodological and procedural point of view is always a positive result, since it provides well-founded knowledge. And this result will in any case be useful for practitioners; it can possibly avert or help to avoid harm for practitioners.

In this respect, scientific work – in advance, so to speak – will make a valuable *contribution* to a practical goal, but it *cannot* achieve that practical goal *itself*.

It cannot be ruled out that the result of the study can be used for subordinate practical objectives – however, the formulated objective of a scientific paper does not state the resulting practical result as an objective, but rather the resulting result of the study.

This argument does not please those in whose fields of study the practical result of a problem solution is always regarded as primary. But would it not be conceivable to change one's own idea of reality to the primarily scientifically oriented approach presented here – and to treat the practical result rather as an addendum, as an appendix or as a possible example of an implementation of the scientific test results?

This might also be a good way for all those part-time students who want to investigate something for their employer and who expect a practical solution from them.

If the focus is on the scientific development of opportunities and risks and if options remain open as to how practical application could now be proceeded further, then the employer himself would have more room for manoeuvre and decision than if he had to approve a meticulously completed concept or product or implementation model.

As is well known, most employers love to choose and make their own decisions on implementation instead of taking over ready-made action processes.

3.3   Primary and Secondary Research

When a researcher generates data himself, i.e. carries out an empirical survey in which he has to count or measure and in which the data he collects himself is processed and statistically evaluated, this is referred to as „primary research".

However, when existing data is processed and statistically evaluated, the term „secondary research" is used.

Both approaches can be regarded as equivalent, because it is far from possible for everyone to collect the necessary data themselves.

Examples of secondary research:

For example, if data on the consumption of plant foods in Germany in the period of the first quarter of the previous year are required, the researcher cannot generate them himself, but must call them up from the corresponding sources.

Another example: to illustrate the CO2 balance of foodstuffs, the economist Tobias Hagen drew on data from the Federal Environment Ministry.

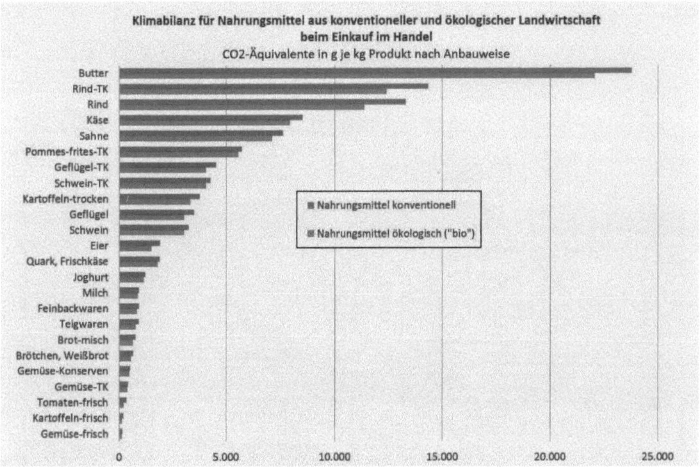

Figure 6: Carbon Footprint of Foodstuffs

(Source: Hagen 2014)

The graph shows that organic food causes fewer climatic effects and that plant food leaves the most favourable climate balance.

3.4 Inductive and Deductive Approach

The word induction here stands for the fact that in an investigation one starts from what is observable and wants to draw conclusions from it. What can be observed is not only facts that can be captured empirically or in everyday life, but also everything that goes into the research project from sources worth quoting.

Inductive approach *(bottom-up)* allows hypotheses and theories to be developed, after which they can be empirically tested deductively *(top-down)* by formulating hypotheses and theories in such a way that they can actually be empirically tested (cf. Popper 1966: 15), using the method of falsification; non falsified components of a hypothesis or theory are assessed as „provisionally confirmed" but not as „verified".

Balzert et al. have developed a helpful model for inductive and deductive research that illustrates the differences and the interaction of induction and deduction.

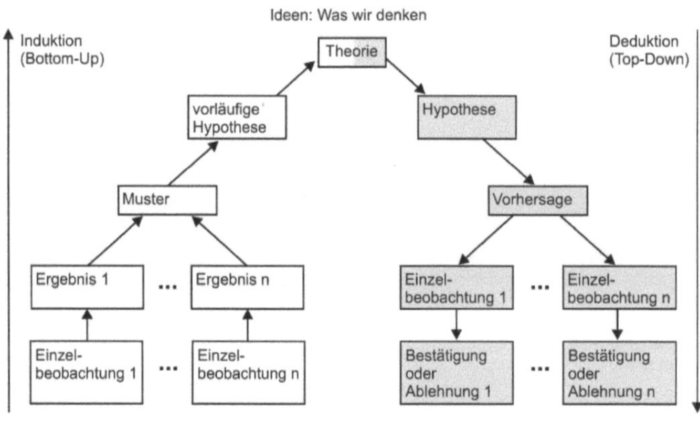

Figure 7: The Induction and Deduction Research Methods

(Source: Balzert et al. 2011: 269)

Translation of words:

Einzelbeobachtung, Ergebnis, Muster,	Individual observation, result, pattern,
vorläufige Hypothese,	preliminary hypothesis,
Theorie,	Theory,
Hypothese, Vorhersage, Einzelbeobachtung, Bestätigung oder Ablehnung	Hypothesis, prediction, individual observation, confirmation or rejection

This model could be supplemented if necessary by a horizontal arrow below, running from right to left, in order to draw attention to the subsequent possibility of using a deductively obtained research result (confirmations, rejections) for renewed or also differently created inductive research.

3.5   Empirical Research

The word empiricism (experience, knowledge of experience) comes from Greek. Whether hypothesis or theory or model: they always need testing and probation in practice, with the help of defined methods. Empirical research projects distinguish between qualitative and quantitative methods.

Characteristics of the Qualitative Approach

Statements, attitudes and opinions are recorded by hermeneutic, but also by narrative and other methods in order to make their meanings usable.

This usually happens with a small number of cases, because qualitative interviews, for example, which consist of open questions and thus sometimes far-reaching answers, are obtained where they are meaningful; frequencies of the same or similar answers usually do not play the main role.

This is a similar procedure to the scientific literature: one looks for statements that could be used as arguments.

As a rule, qualitative surveys are used for inductive research projects.

Characteristics of the Quantitative Approach

Surveys or measurements only record what is countable, measurable or collectable, because the aim here is to generate data that can be statistically evaluated.

In the social sciences, the representativeness of quantitative results is important; therefore, a sample in relation to a population is defined and, as a rule, significantly higher case numbers are required for the investigation than for the qualitative approach.

Quantitative interviews or surveys do not consist of open questions, but of closed questions: respondents can only provide standardized information.

As a rule, quantitative surveys are used for deductive research projects.

Getting Acquainted

A literature tip at this point: If you want to conduct empirical research in the human and social sciences, you cannot ignore the basic work „Research Methods and Evaluation" (Bortz and Döring 2009).

It gives us an overview of empirical research, it leads us from the questioning to the investigation, quantitative and qualitative methods are explained, hypothesis extraction and theory formation, different analysis formats...

Felix Riesenhuber (2009) sketches the situation of the choice of methods for empirical research in a conclusive model that does not require further explanation. For our purposes, we have mirrored the following illustration of his model from the original.

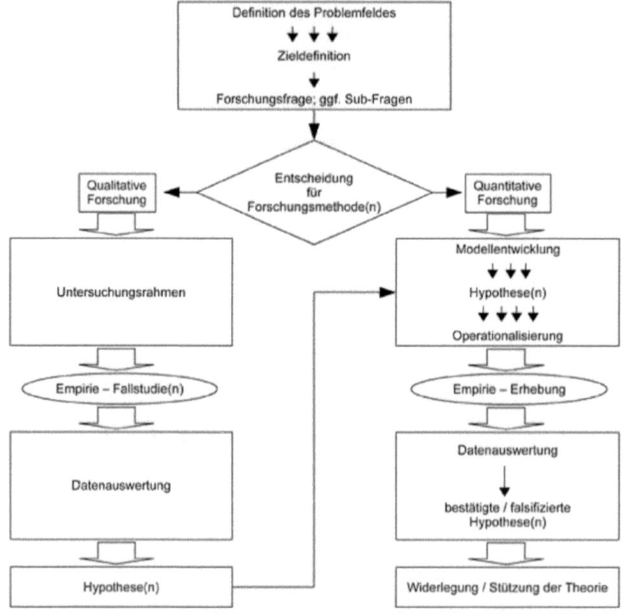

Figure 8: Generic procedure of a research project

(Source: Own presentation based on Riesenhuber 2009: 4)

Translation of words:

	Definition of the problem field	
	Goal definition	
	Research question; possibly sub-questions	
Qualitative research	Decision for research method(s)	Quantitative research
Scope of inquiry		Model development
Empirical Case Studies		Hypothesis(s)
Data analysis		Operationalization
Hypothesis(s)		Empirical survey
		Data analysis
		Confirmed / falsified hypothesis(s)
		Refutation/support of theory

If one now considers the two models for quantitative and qualitative method selection (cf. Fig. 8, Generic procedure of a research project) and for induction and deduction (cf. Fig. 7, The induction and deduction research methods), the question arises as to their relationship.

It can be answered in this way:

- In the *inductive* approach – i.e. the formation of hypotheses and theories – *qualitative* empirical methods will frequently (but not exclusively) be used;

- In the *deductive* approach - i.e. hypothesis and theory testing - *quantitative* empirical methods will frequently (but not exclusively) be used.

Possible Combinations

It can be useful for many research projects and is particularly appreciated in the humanities and social sciences to supplement quantitative surveys with some qualitative components. This is referred to as a partially standardized survey.

The reason for this combined survey form is that in a standardised survey one can only ask what one wants to know in any case; information that deviates from, contradicts or supplements it, i.e. is useful in many cases, cannot benefit a purely quantitative investigation.

A parallel evaluation of the qualitatively collected data, on the other hand, may open up new perspectives that can be incorporated into further phases of the research and promote the self-critical handling of the researcher's own approach.

3.6   Hypotheses

As already explained at the beginning, scientists repeatedly go beyond the boundaries of their own field and then do interdisciplinary research.

This may be due to the fact that only one other scientific discipline has the instruments that can be helpful for its own research question.

In particular, the empirical methods of social science are frequently used by other disciplines to support the respective hypothesis or theory formation or to test a thesis.

Terms

According to Bortz and Döring, these criteria must be met:

- *„A scientific hypothesis refers to real facts that can be empirically examined.*

- *A scientific hypothesis is a generally valid assertion that goes beyond the individual case or a single event ('universal theorem')"* (Bortz and Döring 2009: 4).

Distinctions

Following Bortz and Döring, Riesenhuber differentiates between research hypotheses, operational hypotheses and statistical hypotheses.

- Accordingly, *research hypotheses* refer to relationships in the population to be investigated, about which findings are to be gained by the sample. Three types of hypotheses are to be distinguished: connection hypotheses, difference hypotheses and change hypotheses, where not a generally valid, but a concrete test is to be developed.

- According to Riesenhuber, operationalization follows in the form of an *operational hypothesis* with the definition of the type and path of testing the research hypothesis.

- Finally, *statistical hypotheses* are generated, which are differentiated into null hypotheses and alternative hypotheses and verified by a significance test.

(Cf. Riesenhuber 2009: 8 f. and Bortz and Döring 2009: 492 f.)

Just as the central research question is operationalized by subdividing it into subquestions in more complex research projects, hypotheses must also be operationalized appropriately.

Singular vs. universally valid

In principle, Bortz and Döring maintain that a scientific hypothesis asserts a *generally valid relationship* between several variables, which does not only apply to individual cases of investigation or events (cf. Bortz and Döring 2009: 7).

Balzert and others define this term as follows: *„A hypothesis is an assumption about the connection between at least two facts"* (Balzert and others 2011: 270). A network of coherent, logically contradiction-free statements – from proven hypotheses – then forms a theory of far-reaching explanatory power (cf. Balzert and others 2011: 270); here, too, the implicit orientation is towards a significance beyond the individual case.

If, according to the original Greek meaning for *hypothesis,* this term means an assumption that has not yet been proven, it could also be used for singular assumptions with corresponding, proven references to a more fundamental meaning.

However, in order to avoid conflicts with the common definitions, according to which a hypothesis designates generally valid variable relationships, two helpful ways are possible:

- In singular cases (*"The conversion of the online distribution of long-life vegan food to the ordering system X leads to an increase in turnover in the amount of Y"*) one can work with the term „assumption" instead of „hypothesis".

- One can fall back on the leading research question, which should also have a conditional content („if – then" or „the – the") of its contained variables. For example: *„To what extent can an increase in turnover be expected after the conversion of online distribution of vegan foods with a longer shelf life to the ordering system X"?*

In principle, however, it must be necessary to work empirically and with hypotheses because of the orientation and objectives of your research project. To collect and evaluate data as a proof of your competence in the application of research methods (cf. Karmasin and Ribing 2006: 110) would not yet be a sufficient reason to choose for an empirical approach – from the point of view of a research-oriented introduction to scientific work.

3.7 Significance of the Results

When the scientific work is finally completed, the author is often pleasantly satisfied because he feels that he has made an important, useful and good contribution.

Satisfaction with this is also largely due to the result, which is now believed to have great significance. One is confident to have recognized something new and universal and to have handed it over to one's fellow world.

In addition, a reminder of the video on the fishing net parable by Hans–Peter Dürr is recommendable. Dürr relativized the importance of findings by making it clear that all our scientific knowledge and results are determined solely by the choice of our methods and instruments, so that no generally valid statements can result from them. (Cf. Hans–Peter Dürr in Gertler 1997b from 22:30 to 24:22)

Does that reduce the value of a scientific paper? No – because anyone who researches with this awareness knows that he is always making a current contribution to science and hopefully also to the well-being of his fellow human beings.

It remains to be seen whether this contribution will prove its worth and for whom it can actually be useful, and that ultimately makes research really exciting.

As a rule, the results of a good scientific study make sense, especially if it is illuminating and therefore helpful for a practical problem.

This is what we need to focus on when we are dealing with a topic that we can set for ourselves, such as for final theses, but often also for term papers. The results obtained should then be useful for something.

Especially problems from the areas of the still young vegan economy are on the table and are also very exciting. Because suddenly some previous so-called basic laws of the economy do not function any more. Instead, it is about avoiding and replacing components of animal origin in almost all areas of the value chain, from nutrition – in manufacturing, production and distribution – to clothing, body care products, everyday items, travel ...

Large suppliers in all these areas have long since been focusing on this. They need suitable offers for the demands of their increasing vegan clientele – research is used to find out useful specifications for this goal, and development then follows that research in the preparation of the implementation.

In this respect, more and more scientific work contributes to researching preparatory work for such practical goals.

This is why all scientific work, however small it may be, is of particular importance when it comes to meeting these challenges and delivering results, i.e. creating new knowledge.

Sometimes, however, a great disappointment arises when the scientific work is unexpectedly badly evaluated, and one wonders: Why can my work be badly evaluated because of formulations, formats and insufficient scientific knowledge?

Unscientific language and insufficient use of scientific forms and procedures can lead to a poor assessment and, of course, to „failing“, regardless of the subject matter aspects, in view of the requirements placed on university „scientific products“ – these are, for example, term papers, referees, project papers, theses, actually all objections to be examined at universities.

The essence of a scientific product is its creation with the help of science. Therefore, compliance with scientific quality criteria and scientific methods is indispensable.

„Practical" collations and explanations alone do not, of course, constitute a scientific (i.e. research) achievement – but this is explicitly required in all examination regulations of all universities in Germany. This cannot be otherwise, since universities award scientific degrees; their Master's degrees must also enable doctoral candidates to do their doctorate. Whether they do this is checked by regular accreditations – so it is not only the students who are evaluated and have to meet the requirements of the state and federal level.

These requirements apply equally to universities and universities of applied sciences, because their degrees are equal (in contrast to earlier diplomas etc.) and all courses offered in Germany are also examined and accredited according to identical criteria. This is not the case in all European countries.

Subject-related work is a necessary part of the course of study. However, they can only pass if they have been written in accordance with the requirements for scientific forms of working and the scientific quality criteria.

3.8   Task Sheet for this Chapter

Support your self-study through these tasks!

1. Apply the sketch of research processes presented at the beginning to a project of your choice. Name the problem, define a research goal and design a preliminary research question.

2. Afterwards, you research suitable research methods – for example by searching for similarly related and published studies. Decide and justify your choice.

3. Categorize the research type according to 3.1.

4. Categorize your approach: inductive or deductive?

5. If you need to do an empirical research project: qualitative, quantitative or both? Why?

6. Formulate hypotheses or assumptions that would make sense in your project based on your current level of knowledge and use the notes in 3.6.

7. According to the sketch of research processes presented at the beginning of this chapter, plan now your approach from the perspective: How much time is likely to be available to me – and how much time will I need at least for each of the planned steps, so how much time do I need overall?

4

4 Basic Components

Problem definition, objective and research question are needed to be able to achieve a result of research at all – otherwise no scientific work is created.

You must also be familiar with terms such as hypotheses, criteria and characteristics.

Above all, the formulation of the topic must be consistent!

4.1   Subject

A scientific „product" (homework, project work, final theses, etc.) can be identified by a suitable title, It must make it clear in a few, clear words which problem is being tackled.

Complete sentences and question or exclamation marks are inappropriate (this also applies to all headings within the assignment).

The naming of concrete companies or cases is to be avoided, because otherwise in case of unexpected changes on the part of those involved, a change of the announced topic could become necessary, which is not, however, still possible at any university at any time.

The title names the key points of the project in as concise a form as possible. The contained keywords (preferably only three - for better memorability) must of course also be found in the structure of the work, i.e. in the headings.

The necessary dependencies or references of the keywords, which are defined in the research question concretizing the topic, can already be recognized from the title.

Examples of clear, therefore good formulations:

- Business plan factors for a vegan online shop
- Opportunities and risks of a campaign against environmentally hazardous livestock farming
- Characteristics of a communication strategy for the exploitation of the omnivores in the generation 55plus

Examples of too complex, therefore unclear formulations:

- Investigation of approaches for the registration of company and brand identities for the realization of a brand image for a new vegan retail chain
- Value-based approaches for the identification, measurement and presentation of customer value as a reflection of the valuation of intangible assets
- Creating new worlds of experience in music – applying semantic technologies to complex data structures using the example of audio files

Examples of meaningless, therefore unusable formulations:

- Vegans on the web
- Vegan can do everything – but who can live vegan?
- Beautiful new world of veganism

The two areas described as negative examples make it clear: we need concise and clear formulations of topics which everyone can immediately imagine and which can also be redeemed.

Topics that contain a phrase „using the example of…" are unsuitable, because not only every medical or criminalistic, but also every scientific investigation can only examine concrete things and can only arrive at concrete results, but not at generally valid statements. Thus, the „example" should be reformulated as the actual object or place of investigation.

This is realizable in the twinkling of an eye: Instead of „success factors for vegane Onlineshops at the example of smilefood.de", the title would have to be formulated correctly: „success factors for the vegan onlineshop smilefood.de".

At the end of the path, every work is not only measured by whether a problem has been identified, a clear objective defined and a feasible – operationalisable – research question formulated, but also whether the topic of the work has been met!

The title is on the cover page – and it must have been realized, otherwise all effort has been wasted.

4.2   Problem Definition

Problem definition and objective definition – both must be worked on in order to be able to do research at all. Below are five examples of how to deal with these terms.

Most problems are still of a general nature, although they have already arisen oriented towards a concrete problem.

Remember: you have to research towards an objective, that has to be a contribution for solving a specific problem!

Examples:

1. Organic vegan cultivation of fruit and vegetables should take place without fertilisation with animal components and without chemical treatment – but in the specific case of a site X this is not possible year after year.

2. Organic vegan crops are expected to be available in greater quantities at farm X than is needed in the surrounding area – overproduction must be prevented in order to avoid bankruptcy of the company.

3. The dry preliminary products for the realization of vegan slices of the mark X consist of dried, extruded soy – soy products are however increasingly not tolerated by some humans and/or due to the image discredited in some media increasingly less accepted by customers, therefore the sales decreases.

4. A vegan restaurant is to be built; however, vegan restaurants in this city always suffer after some time existence-threatening declines in

demand.

5. There is currently no vegan nursing home within a radius of over 200 kilometres, but demand is increasing.

4.3 Definition of Objectives

Objectives are more concrete than the previously identified problems and take into account more details, such as local and temporal circumstances.

Examples:

1. Find out which types of fruit and vegetables could be cultivated organically at site X.

2. Find out which additional distribution possibilities could be possible and profitable for how much of the harvest of farm X.

3. Find out which alternative purely vegetable ingredients could be processed into comparable dry intermediates with the same benefits.

4. Find out which target groups would deal more sustainably with which vegan offers of a restaurant.

5. Find out which criteria a vegan nursing home would have to fulfil and which current operators would set up such a facility.

In the synopsis of the problem and the objective, it becomes clear that they build on each other and, by focusing on the objective, open the way to the drafting of even more concrete research questions.

So far it has only been determined – from one's own perception or that of a potential client – which deficit exists and why it should be possible to remedy it and with what objective.

Before we take the next step to develop the associated research questions, it would now make sense to formulate conceivable search questions for each of the five examples. In any case, you have to do more research in order to move from the objective to the research question.

4.4 Research Question

An indispensable component of any scientific assignment is the formulation of the central research question. Those who merely „illuminate" their „subject" may write an essay, but not yet a scientific paper. Rather, a research question is posed there - in the form of a question sentence. This leads to analytical steps, argumentations and the use of defined methods.

No research goal can be achieved without a research question. And so it is not surprising that no peer-reviewed journal today will accept an article without a qualified „key research question". From the introduction, where it is to be formulated in a well-founded and comprehensible manner, the research question must be latently drawn like a „red thread" through the text of the paper – and it must be mentioned again and explicitly answered in the last chapter of the paper, the conclusion or the concluding discussion.

Development of a Research Question

The research question is not yet fixed at the very beginning of a scientific knowledge process, but is developed or specified only after initial literature and data studies. Without research of this kind, a research question cannot yet be posed.

In the case of more extensive work, it can be differentiated into partial questions if necessary. In the course of the research process, it is then further specified – and conclusively answered at the end of the work.

The description of the procedure must be explained in conjunction with the research question or the research sub-questions. All this is done in the introductory chapter of a scientific paper, which is best not entitled „Introduction", but more clearly „Problem, objective and research question".

Ask correctly

How can you narrow down your research question so that it can be conclusively answered within the given time frame and scope of the work? Research questions such as *„Is the implementation of an online shop worthwhile for our vegan products"* are unsuitable, because such questions could only be answered with yes or no and do not indicate a recognizable research direction.

A research question can also not be an open-ended question, because you have to sketch out a path, by expressing *conditions* between variables, as they can be recognized by formulations such as: „Under what conditions...", „Under what conditions must be...", „In what respect and to what extent...", etc.

A research question operationalises the path necessary for reaching the goal. From it one can understandably infer, which way the investigation will take and must take.

Falling back on what has previously been investigated

We could only draft our research question for the time being, because the existing scientific and professional literature would have to be looked at first. Possibly there would already be answers to the concrete problems and objectives – then no investigation would be necessary at first. Or there would be found some hints and results which would now have to be used for the formulation of the research question and thus for the processing of the „red thread".

Implementation using Examples

Prior to this, we had already compiled five different problems and formulated the appropriate objectives, and by omitting the literature research and review that was actually necessary in the first place, the first research questions are now to be formulated:

Examples:

1. To what extent, with what varieties and at what intervals can organic vegan fruit and vegetables be cultivated at site X?

2. To what extent can which parts of the harvest of farm X be offered profitably through which distribution channels?

3. Which purely vegetable and continuously available ingredients, apart from soya, can be processed to what extent and with what profitability into comparable dry intermediates in accordance with the standards of the X brand and with the same benefits?

4. To what extent would which target groups in the city of X deal with a vegan buffet offer, a defined multi-course menu or an a la carte offer?

5. Which relevant criteria would a vegan nursing home at location X have to fulfil?

The research questions drafted here are not yet sharpened by research in research literature. It should become clear, however, that only existing scientific literature, preliminary investigations and elements of the respective objective that can be investigated with scientific methods should be included in research questions – hence the omission of the potential operators of an old people's home mentioned in the objective for example 5, for which not a scientific investigation would be necessary, but only research, after the investigation has been completed.

We also and above all learn from negative examples. Only when our ideas of reality do not work, do we wake up, scratch our heads and say: „Oh, I have to take another closer look..." – so our everyday experience.

Therefore we should now also treat negative examples. For each example there is an indication as to why it must be a negative example:

Examples:

1. How can organic vegan cultivation of fruit and vegetables be carried out at site X?

2. Can the harvest results of farm X be offered profitably?

3. Which purely vegetable ingredients can be processed into comparable dry precursors?

4. What has the best chances: a buffet offer, a multi-course menu or an a–la–carte offer?

5. What should a vegan nursing home at location X look like?

I have these criticism:

1. The obvious answer: Well, in a hundred thousand different ways, perhaps... So: not a focused, operationalizable question.

2. There are only two answers: yes or no.

3. Spontaneous answer: Sooo many... – this is again not a question focused on a concrete object of investigation.

4. Answer: Too open, too vague, not examinable.

5. Cheeky answer: in any case painted green!

It is therefore clear that research questions must be developed with care, derived from the objectives of the research project.

4.5   Further Instruments

The use of *hypotheses* requires that a general validity of the results can be expected, otherwise one should better speak of *assumptions*, as explained in chapter 3.6.

Two publications should be mentioned at this point:

- The development of hypotheses and their verification as well as the collection and evaluation of qualitative and quantitative data are dealt with in the standard work „Forschungsmethoden und Evaluation für Human- und Sozialwissenschaftler" (cf. Bortz and Döring 2009). If you need to conduct empirical research, you should base your own approach and choice of method on these basic principles.

- In 2009, Riesenhuber briefly described the formation of hypotheses in the fundamentals of large-scale empirical research, which can also be a valuable source for prospective empiricists (cf. Riesenhuber 2009).

According to Bortz and Döring, hypotheses are to be formulated in this way:

- *„A scientific hypothesis must at least implicitly be based on the formal structure of a meaningful conditional sentence ('if... then... sentence' or 'the... the... sentence').*

- *The conditional sentence must be potentially falsifiable, i.e. events must be conceivable that could contradict that conditional sentence"* (Bortz and Döring 2009: 4).

When developing hypotheses, care must be taken to assign the independent variable to the *if* part and the dependent variable to the *then* part.

- *Example: If someone buys products containing animal ingredients, he pays for the suffering and murder of animals.*

A the-thesentence is formulated when variables are created quantitatively.

- *Example: The broader the product range of a vegan online shop, the smaller the outflow of regular customers.*

Criteria, characteristics and *values* are further important terms in scientific investigations.

- Criteria are to be understood here as serving for differentiation or selection, but not synonymous with characteristics (cf. Duden 2013a);

- Characteristics are understood as distinguishing signs or characteristics by which persons, groups, things or states can be recognized (cf. Duden 2013b).

- Values are understood as concretisations of the occurrence of the characteristics.

Examples:

1. If the changes in the body weight of a person since switching to vegan nutrition are to play a role as a *criterion* for changes through vegan nutrition, their body weight is the necessary *characteristic* for this and the exact kg data are the *values*. Here one speaks of quantitative characteristics.

2. If as *criterion* of a vegan meal it is to be considered that no components of animal origin are contained, one will make sure before taking the meal that the recognizable or also measurable *characteristics* of the components can be concluded all on purely vegetable origin. In such cases one speaks of qualitative or categorical characteristics, the expressions will be here namely categorical kind: Fruit, vegetables, cereals etc.

   However, if there is reason to determine the existing proportion of animal constituents, quantitative characteristics will be used, such as weight, volume or percentage of animal constituents.

3. The use of these terms also makes sense for studies which are not empirical and for which no statistical data preparation takes place. In the case of a research question such as „In what respect and to what extent can the supplementation of vitamin B12 in person X contribute to an improvement in health?" one is challenged to assign comprehensible characteristics to the target criterion „health improvement" and to explain and justify their characteristics. Furthermore, for the questionnaire components „In what respect and to what extent" criteria will also have to be applied, and even the "supplementation" will probably have to be documented with a quantitative characteristic.

The inclusion of the terms „criterion", „characteristic" and „value" in our personal toolbox for scientific work can thus help us to deal with the content components of a subject in an orderly manner and to take up the interrelationships between them.

The same also applies to the term *variable*, which is used in the statistics for the transfer of characteristics (cf. on the connection between the terms characteristic and variable: Hennecke et al. 2001).

4.6   Task Sheet for this Chapter

Support your self-study through these tasks!

1. Apply the suggestions presented at the beginning for a clear and comprehensible topic formulation to a project of your choice. Pay attention to key concepts that form part of the structure, the problem definition, the research objective and the research question.

2. Then, based on your current level of knowledge, determine a problem, an objective, and a preliminary research question according to the examples in the lesson.

3. Formulate hypotheses or assumptions that would make sense in your project based on your current level of knowledge, and use the notes in 4.5.

4. Finally, check the previous steps in this chapter for coherence and consistency and, if possible, share your notes with someone who was not previously involved with your research idea, and ask him for feedback.

5 Scientific Sources

Different requirements apply to scientific work than to practical assignments in everyday professional life. Scientific work can only be scientific if it is based on sources worth quoting and referenced in the correct form

This chapter is intended to provide answers and hints to the most frequently asked questions on how to deal with sources.

Scientific texts differ from other text genres by the indispensable requirement that all external statements must be documented in a comprehensible and verifiable manner. Both the literal as well as the analogous adoption of foreign thoughts must be made recognisable by unambiguous references. If these references are missing, one is inevitably guilty of plagiarism.

What do we actually need references for? It's that others can clearly find the exact place of a foreign text that we need for our argumentation where we found it ourselves, using the bibliographic data of the original work and the exact page numbers.

There are different conventions and styles for the design of such references, be it the complete bibliographic information or the short references, whether recorded in a footnote or in the text.

The usual forms are the American APA and Harvard systems, both of which work with short references in parentheses. In the current text – i.e. not in a footnote – the author's name, year of publication and page number are indicated in parentheses before or directly at the end of a literal or non-literal quote.

The indication for indirect quotations, i.e. quotations combined in one's own words, is introduced with „cf." (= compare). If several publications by the same author from the same year are used, they are distinguished by „a", „b", „c" etc. in addition to the year: 2018a, 2018b etc.

The complete bibliographic informations appear only in the bibliography.

5.1   Search and find

Three types of scientific literature can be identified: Primary sources in the sense of original scientific literature, Secondary sources such as bibliographies or library catalogues, and Tertiary sources such as dictionaries, manuals or textbooks (cf. Brink 2005: 49).

It might be helpful to inventorise literature in this way: First the topicality is checked, then the author of the text with regard to further specialist achievements, then the disciplinary perspective of the text is determined and clarified, which question underlies it, and finally it is classified to which category the text is to be counted – dissertation or journal article or monographical work or similar (cf. Frank et al. 2007: 33 f.).

In so-called online databases you will find mainly current scientific literature, especially in the form of journal articles. For research in such online databases, enter author names, complete book titles, title keywords or keywords; if a term is entered in the singular, versions in the plural are usually not output (cf. Bünting et al. 2008: 59).

In Internet searches, you choose either the pattern method or the semantic method. With the pattern method, you enter a keyword – the more general, the more hits are displayed. With the semantic method, several terms are used to create content-related connections; this will make a search more successful (see Bünting et al. 2008: 60).

5.2   Excerpting

When reviewing literature, it is useful and helpful to prepare extracts by yourself – whether you will use them afterwards or not.

This could be done in this way:

- In the header you note the date of excerpting, the bibliographic data of the text, the location and a summary of the text.

- The main part contains the questions of the text, paraphrases (always written in subjunctive), possibly literal quotations, references to the literature and own ideas, comments as well as cross-references.

- The footer contains information about the importance of what has been read, the place and type of further processing.

(Cf. Bünting et al. 2008: 34 f.)

Excerpts can also be stored in the literature management program of your choice – my recommendation: Zotero.

5.3   Citation Formats

The citation form for literal / direct quotations must be distinguished from the specification for non-literal / indirect or analogous quotations.

The *direct quotation* is the literal adoption of a text passage. Such quotations must be literally accurate, even errors of the original must be taken over. Any omissions from the original are indicated by square brackets „[...]“ and any additions in the quotation are also enclosed in square brackets.

However, literal quotes should only be used extremely rarely; a scientific work is simply not a poetry album. Only if you can't quote something better or more appropriately that someone has published somewhere, use a literal quote – for example in definitions or prominent statements (by Einstein etc.).

In all other cases, the source text is summarized in indirect speech, i.e. in the subjunctive, without, of course, omitting any relevant content.

Short quotations can be inserted into the text by quotation marks, longer literal quotations – i.e. longer than three lines – can be highlighted by indentation, and the source is indicated directly after each quotation in the form of a short reference.

The basically rather rare literal quotations are thus recognizable in the text by the quotation marks and are directly referenced.

Example:

„Many people, even most, think that in conflict situations, the interests of us humans are more important than those of animals – so much more so that almost everything seems permissible with animals“ (Sezgin 2014).

If you only use a short literal quote, it can also appear in your own text.

Example:

Hilal Sezgin underlines that people value their own interests so much more than those of animals,“that almost everything seems to be allowed with animals“ (Sezgin 2014).

In an indirect speech, the quote might look like this:

Example:

According to Sezgin, most people think that their own interests have priority over those of animals, so that virtually all procedures are allowed (see Sezgin 2014).

If footnotes are used instead of in-text references, the same difference applies: in the case of literal quotations, the footnote refers directly to the source; in the case of non-literal quotations, it begins with „Compare" (Cf.) before the source reference.

Long citations with detailed information about the source can no longer be used – the short citations shown above are now common in footnotes or in the text.

5.4   Online Sources

This also applies to Internet sources. URL information does not belong in the footnotes or in the documents in the text, but is provided with meaningful information such as references to print sources. In the meantime, printed and online sources have been entered together in the „bibliography".

In the text of the scientific paper, short references then look like this:

a) ...in footnotes:

1   Cf. Gertler 2011b, p. 18

2   Cf. Gertler 2011a

Since a URL source does not know page numbers (except: PDF), you do not need to specify a page number in the footnote here.

If you set In-Text short references instead of footnotes, the short references are in parentheses, before the concluding point and under lower case of the cf. reference, as implemented in this note: (cf. Gertler 2011b: 18).

Why do footnotes usually appear like this „..., p. 18", but for in-the-text referencing „...: 18"? Such footnotes follow the output form of APA, where the time number is preceded by „S." in German; when in-the-text referencing follows the Harvard citation style, only a colon in the short reference refers to the following page number.

b) ...in the bibliography:

Gertler, M. (2011a): Journalistische Wirklichkeitsangebote, available at: http://hcri.de/archives/196 [retrieved 22 October 2014].

Gertler, M. (2011b): Zwischen Ökonomie und Ethik: Zur Qualität in Theorie und Praxis des Journalismus: Munich: GRIN Verlag GmbH.

A look at the list of sources, the bibliography, reveals which source is available in printed form and which comes from the Internet. In fact we treat both sources in the same way – after all, we do not distinguish in the text part of the work whether the respective source is used printed or online available.

5.5   Wrong Sources

Again and again statistics are needed for the argumentation. It is important to note that the supplier of such statistics, e.g. Statista, is sometimes not even the author and source of the data to which we refer.

Statista even refers to this in its own tips (cf. Statista 2013). As a rule, Statista only provides the service of processing data of third parties into usable tables/graphics. Therefore, this citation method - example taken from the Statista tip page - applies:

Allensbach Institute for Public Opinion Research (2013): Allensbacher Computer- und Technik-Analyse – ACTA 2013; 2009 to 2013, quoted according to de.statista.com, URL http://de.statista.com/statistik/daten/studie/168741/umfrage/interesse-der-bevoelkerung-an-fitness/, retrieved 16.12.2013, 4.39 p.m.

Quote in the continuous text: (Institut für Demoskopie Allensbach, 2006).

It follows that information in the bibliography, footnotes or in-text references of a work may not begin with the author reference „Statista", unless it is the publication of a statistic whose author is Statista himself.

The same applies analogously to references to Facebook profiles, groups or pages, and of course to any video deposited on YouTube or Vimeo etc. All these platforms are not themselves the authors of the respective media products, but merely serve to disseminate content for which others are responsible.

Only where the platform operator „speaks" himself is he the „speaker" and can be quoted as such.

5.6   Quotable and Worth Quoting

„Quotable" are sources that can be verified because they have been published regularly and are therefore available in libraries or online.

The possibility of viewing theses in a local university library, for example, does not replace publication; such academic products cannot be ordered via inter-library loan. Thus, there is no availability for everyone. Strict adherence to the

„citation capability" is indispensable for achieving the scientific quality criterion of verifiability.

Sources that are to be used must be published in any case - then they are to be classified as citable. If this is not the case, for example in specially conducted interviews or information carried out by third parties, these sources must be documented in the appendix of the paper and thus published and made citable within the framework of the paper itself.

This also means that term papers and theses that may be accessible in the university library cannot be cited because they are not published and therefore not accessible to third parties. The scientific quality criterion of „verifiability" is not satisfied by the fact that a thesis is only „publicly accessible", for example in the library of a single university. This is because unpublished (!) theses are not accessible via automated inter-library loan.

„Published", on the other hand, means that it is available also beyond a local institution – in the book trade, in various libraries as well as via interlibrary loan or can be retrieved online. In the case of this thesis, this would only be the case if it would been published by an appropriate publisher.

Anyone who quotes content from a diploma thesis (which is only accessible locally) and uses it as a source will inevitably be told by the examiner that this is a source that cannot be quoted because it has not been published - even if it may be worth quoting.

All sources must be verifiable and controllable, used quotations must be comparable to the original.

As a rule, only scientific sources as well as information published by organisations and companies on matters affecting them themselves are considered *„worth quoting"* – but not journalistic or entertaining products.

Public journals and other non-scientific literature are generally not considered worth quoting; they cannot be used for scientific argumentation. Journalistic products and entertainment products are by nature not scientific products.

Among the non-scientific sources is also the online encyclopedia Wikipedia, as no scientific responsibility is guaranteed there.

There are these exceptions:

- Non-scientific literature can be referenced to a limited extent in the „discovery context" (introduction with problem, objective and research question, etc.), if necessary also selectively in the main part for the mere presentation of published opinions / information, but not for the actual argumentation in the work.

- Non-scientific literature can be used and referenced if (only) the unedited statement of a scientist has been published there (e.g. by interview or in the form of a contribution under his own name).

- Non-scientific literature should of course be used and referenced if it is itself the subject of investigation.

- Professionally / technically relevant publications of organisations and associations (especially statistics, annual reports, statements) can and must be used and cited – if it is necessary to achieve the objectives.

5.7   No „unnamed" Sources

A website without an author's name is not worth quoting, especially because scientific and professional sources always have information about the author or publisher.

If you can't identify an author – for example at https://business.pinterest.com/de/pinterest-analytics – then you will of course name the publisher who is usually listed in the imprint.

Pinterest publishes in German, therefore an imprint is available there. Since it is a publishing company, the company name Pinterest is entered as the author.

The indication „without author" therefore never exists. If really no author or publisher can be found, it will not be a source worth quoting anyway.

5.8   Avoid Plagiarism

It is absolutely necessary to make the references to each source clear in your own contents, because passages with knowledgeable contents, which however could hardly originate from the author of this scientific paper, lead immediately to the suspicion of plagiarism.

It is therefore advisable to begin the passage to be referenced with an introduction similar to this example and then to continue writing:

> *„In his work ABC, the XYZ scientist Max Mustermann argues on this question as follows: There could not be flying cows, simply because... It would also be contrary to the laws of nature, the... In addition, recent studies had come to the conclusion that... In his opinion and in accordance with the laws of logic... In addition, Mustermann sums up that... Mustermann vehemently denies furthermore the possibility... Incidentally, it is a question of methodology..."*

The final footnote is created according to APA-modified: „Cf. Mustermann 2011, p. 87" – or it is referenced in brackets according to Harvard in the text: „(cf. sample man 2011: 87)" – depending on the chosen citation method.

If the foreign content is identified in indirect speech due to the clear formulations, references to a source may also be valid and comprehensible across several paragraphs.

It should therefore be made clear at the beginning that from now on external contents are reproduced or summarised – and finally make it clear with the concrete reference to the source that this now ends.

It is important to identify all external content and indicate the sources: for texts, illustrations and photos, and above all also for any external thought processes.

Graphics and tables can be transferred directly or indirectly (cf. Karmasin and Ribing 2006: 103). In the case of direct transfer, the form and content of the image are copied without modification, e.g. by scanning and pasting, with source information appearing under the image according to the pattern of all short references: last name, year, page number.

If illustrations have been modified, the source information is: Illustration based on last name, year, page number or source.

5.9   Illustration and Tables

Which information belongs under a figure or a table?

Step 1: Ensure a meaningful label! Insert the image or table into your Word document. By right-clicking on the activated element you can then select: „Insert caption...". Now enter a brief, comprehensible description, as you would for headings. Example: „Sales development 2004 to 2014". This title then appears automatically in the corresponding directory (for figures or tables), retaining the automatic numbering („Figure 3" or „Table 3").

Step 2: Ensure the exact source reference! Do not insert the source reference into the description text of the illustration, but below the illustration into the first following text line, and from there you refer to the source in the form of the short reference. Example: „Source: Müller 2014: 38". If this text line is too far away from the label, you can reduce the „paragraph distance (pt)" appropriately in the formatting palette.

This source must, of course, be listed in the correct form in the bibliography if it is an external source. If you work with a literature management program such as Zotero, this is guaranteed.

If, on the other hand, your insertion is a complete representation of your own, write in the text line below the illustration: „Source: Own representation"; logically there will be no entry in the source directory, which, as is well known, may *only contain published material.*

If, however, you have created your own table that contains parts of a presentation that has already been published somewhere, the information is: „Source: Own presentation based on XYZ", in the form of a short reference.

Source references and short references do not belong in the tables and tables directories – therefore it is necessary to create a separate line below the label.

5.10   Valid Approach

Correct citation requires a lot of attention and thoroughness. There is a great risk that inaccuracies and gaps will lead to the scientific nature of one's own work not being adhered to. Therefore, further hints on constantly occurring small and large individual questions follow.

Can two different sources be referenced within a sentence?

This is easy to solve. You refer to both sources at the end of the sentence in a footnote or in an in-text reference.

In the course of the sentence you make it absolutely clear which content comes from whom: „Meier came to the conclusion in 2011 that... – Müller, however, already questioned this in 2012 through his research result, according to which...". This is the reference for this example: „Cf. Meier 2011: 38 and Müller 2012: 56 f."

This is easy to solve. At the end of the sentence, you refer to both sources in a footnote or in an in-text reference.

In the course of the sentence you make it clear which content comes from whom: „In 2011 Meier came to the conclusion that ... – Müller, however, already questioned this in 2012 with his research result, according to which...".

This is the reference for this example: "Cf. Meier 2011: 38 and Müller 2012: 56 f.".

If, for example, you could only obtain information about the corporate structures for your scientific work from the company's intranet, proceed as follows:

- You save yourself a document by „printing as PDF" or by taking a screenshot, which you keep in the appendix of your research paper.

- In the footnote you then refer as follows: „Cf. statement ABC, retrieved from the company intranet on [date], visible in the appendix under XYZ".

In this way, you have ensured that the unpublished source has become verifiable.

Orally received information usable?

Such questions keep coming up: „What do I write in the footnote and in the bibliography when I have been told orally about a definition by a person of a company and I have written it down? This definition is only used because there is no definition in the literature and my thesis needs this definition of the company".

The answer is clear: If oral information is to be used, it will not find a place in the list of sources, since it cannot be checked anywhere. But of course it must be referenced in the footnote or in the in-text reference, for example: „Personal Message from Manfred Mustermann dated 12.03.2015" or „Answer from Manfred Mustermann in Interview dated 12.03.2015".

In the list of sources, indicate publications with ISSN numbers?

ISSN are the standard numbers for serial publications used to identify series and journals.

Since we only keep a single list of sources and do not separate printed and online sources, the way of citation – omitting the ISSN, as we do not list the ISBN in the directory – is based on the standards.

These basic pattern looks like this:

> Author's last name / A. [for author's first name] (year): Title of article – subtitle of article if applicable In: Series title or official journal abbreviation (issue number if applicable), pp. 123 – 321.

Since all ISSN-captured series are immediately identifiable on the basis of the information on series titles or abbreviations, verifiability is given:

> Gertler, M. (1999): Von der Wirklichkeit überholt. Zur Praxis der Gottesdienstübertragungen im Fernsehen. In: FunkKorrespondenz 47(1999)17, pp. 3 – 7.

The sequence of numbers „47(1999)17“ states: This is the 47th edition in the year 1999, when the 17th volume was published.

Book with a list of sources, but without citations – a usable source?

If readers of a text cannot clearly distinguish where the author of the „citation-free“ book himself argues and where he uses texts, contents or even thoughts of others, you cannot use the book as a source – especially since it does not contain page numbers for the presumed external sources in the text. Such could be classified as plagiarism because the external content could not be identified. This also applies to books from other countries – because the requirement of identification applies internationally.

The distinction between primary literature and secondary literature, which is necessary for you yourself, makes things even more difficult: the ominous book lists sources and presumably books or papers with them in terms of content, but does not make them recognizable – therefore it would be indistinguishable whether you would take up the ideas of third parties (secondary sources) or those of the book author (primary source) if you were using this book as a source. And as we all know, in principle we only work with primary sources.

By omitting footnotes or references in the text, the author of that book has not made his „work“ verifiable throughout - and this alone does not meet the international quality criteria of scientific work. Conclusion: Not usable as a source under any circumstances, not worth quoting!

Double reference a direct quote within an indirect quote?

If it is a clear text paragraph in your work that indicates at the beginning where the non-verbal quotation begins (example: „XY argues that it does not...“), and if your text paragraph ends with the associated reference in the footnote (example: „Cf. XY 2009: 48“), and if the literal quotation contained in your text paragraph (e.g. a short, concise formulation of XY) can also be found on page 48 - within the original passage you did not quote literally - then it is sufficient to end the paragraph with a reference according to the footnote example „Cf. XY 2009: 48“.

However, if the situation is not so clear, you must also reference the literal quotation with a separate footnote (and there without the addition „Cf.“).

Citation of company websites

Usually, we state the author of each quotation. However, if a company website is to be referenced, it is usually not known who wrote the text published online. So the question arises whether the company should be treated as a publisher instead of as an author, and whether "Ed." should also appear in the short title behind the company name.

Each website or web page must be cited by author (if designated) or by publisher (if designated; otherwise use imprint) and thus also sorted in the source list: author / publisher, year of publication, website title.

Therefore, the publisher of the website is entered if no other author is named on the respective individual page.

Can textbooks generally not be quoted? Are there exceptions?

An educational textbook, handbook or compendium cannot usually be cited, because they normally belong to the genre secondary literature: only or predominantly doctrinal opinions or results of other scientists are collected and reproduced there. Remember: only primary literature is to be used for scientific work!

Of course, there are exceptions:

- If in a textbook the editor of the textbook presents his own doctrinal opinion or research results, which were not previously published anywhere else, then these passages may be quoted – at least in those places they are primary literature.

  To the way of implementation: I assume that the textbook author presents two different models of third parties and explains their possible uses; the students have to present the model they want to use in relation to the model author and refer to this primary literature; however, they are welcome to write and discuss in addition that in textbook XYZ this model is evaluated in this way and described in the context of other models to be named in this way and in this case they refer to this textbook passage.

- If a manual (example: „Handbuch Medienethik" by Schicha / Brosda) is in fact a „compilation" – recognizable by the addendum „(Hrsg.)" – in which different specialist authors from their research areas, in which they also otherwise publish scientifically, present essential or perspective in their contributions, these contributions can also be used and cited like those of other compilations.

5.11   Task Sheet for this Chapter

Support your self-study through these tasks!

1. Check the standards for the design of references, such as APA or Harvard, and find out what standards your own university or the publisher or publication series follows, for which you want to prepare a contribution.

2. Once your literature research has started, be sure to always – if possible – use primary sources.

3. Extract for yourself a work file, containing the information and exact locations you are likely to use for your research project.

4. When posting information on platforms such as Statista, YouTube, Facebook, etc., be sure to include the exact author.

5. Make the necessary distinction between „quotable" and „worthy of quotation" your own.

6. Internet sources are to be treated formally like print sources – so do not set any source-related URL information in the text.

7. Avoid plagiarisms by always making it clear where exactly the foreign text begins and where it ends.

8. Also pay attention to the necessary source information in illustrations and tables and avoid these source information appearing in the description text of the illustration or table in the manner described.

6 Literature Management

Even the very first preparations for a scientific paper are about searching for and dealing with existing literature. Nothing would have been as unsuccessful as a mere look around, without capturing more precisely and recording which source you encountered where and why it could possibly be important for the project.

So there is a lot to be said for purchasing a large box of index cards in order to store all the information there in such a way that it can be quickly found and used – whether in this or in the scientific work after next.

Well, of course this does not mean a card index box in the literal sense. It used to be the instrument of choice for these purposes. You could quickly find and use your stored information according to the speed usual at that time - today nothing works without computers.

6.1   Data Generation

Literature management in the computer is similar to the card index – but much more convenient.

You have to fill out index cards manually – this works the same way in Word, the software offers the possibility to enter and manage sources in the toolbox with „Quotes" and to use them for the source directory.

The index box model offers MS Word in this way: By entering the necessary data for each source, a data record is created which is then used as a short reference according to the selected output format – i.e. in the text directly next to the quotation – as well as in the source list: the bibliography.

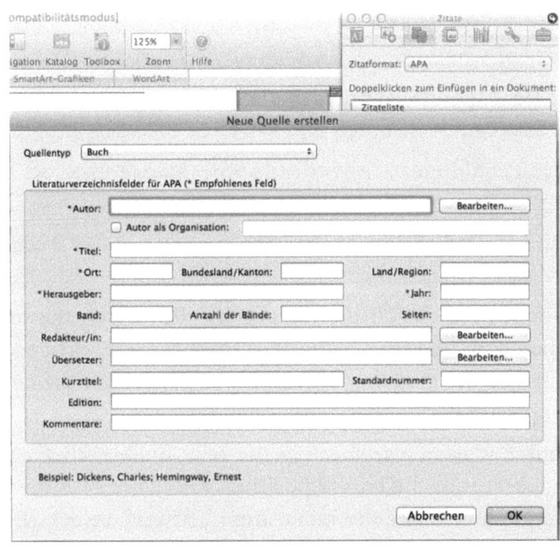

Figure 9: Source Input in MS Word

(Source: own screenshot)

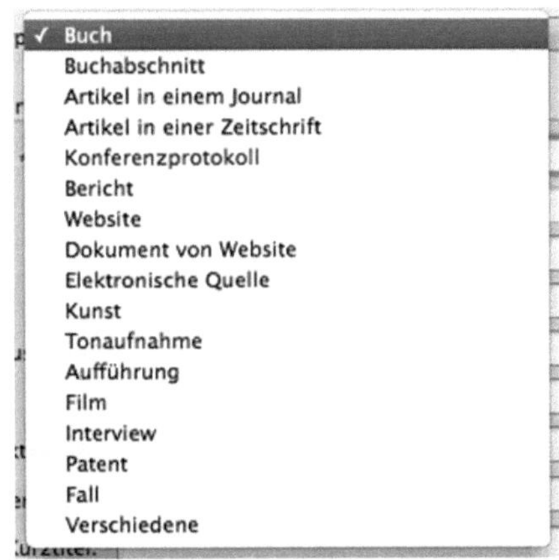

Figure 10: Source Types in MS Word

(Source: own screenshot)

So here you can choose what kind of source it is – a book, a book section, an article, a website or whatever.

Afterwards, at least the information marked with an asterisk must be entered so that source data can be recorded and stored in the write program itself.

For example, you could create a Word file with source excerpts and use them later in your actual work.

Of course, this recording of data in the „index cards" of MS Word could also be done while writing the paper itself.

At the end of each quote, open the toolbox by clicking on the toolbox icon in the standard menu bar and the second icon from the left, click on the plus sign at the bottom left of the toolbox, then an input mask with the necessary fields for the source appears.

If the same source is used elsewhere in the text, double-click on the entry in the toolbox to insert it at the cursor position. Finally, create the source directory, the bibliography: Under the menu item „Insert" select „Document elements" and then „Bibliography".

OpenOffice also offers under „Extras" the item „Literature database", which must also be maintained manually.

So far, today's electronic versions of the good old card index are available to everyone.

If you like to assemble things yourself and don't like to rely on automation, you might want to work with it and find pleasure in it – even a homemade hat is something self-made – so these things have their charm.

However, you have to be sober: this kind of handwork is flawed, because if we ourselves have to search for the necessary information in the book, anthology or magazine article in order to then enter it not with copy & paste, but from our own short-term memory – just read, already typed – it takes a lot of time and causes typing errors.

6.2   Common Data

If perhaps it should not be the hand-written electronic index card, then other proven ways are waiting for us, namely data collections of printed and electronic publications as well as the associated data formats, which enable a fast exchange and a fast transfer of all necessary data to our sources. Special file formats have been developed for exchange and transfer.

Some of these data collections can be „fed" and used by users themselves, others are provided and maintained by university libraries, and finally there are also some that are supplied with data from different libraries.

A good example for such a service is the free BibSonomy. Even without being registered and logged in as a user, you can retrieve all entries from sources that have been approved by the users. Search possibilities by name, place or keyword make finding the source easier.

The search for „Martin Gertler" plus the tag „vegan" led to a result. Suppose someone wants to quote from this e-book, he does not have to manually copy the required information into his electronic index card, but can choose an output format in which he would like to have the data output in order to save it to himself and use it in a literature management program.

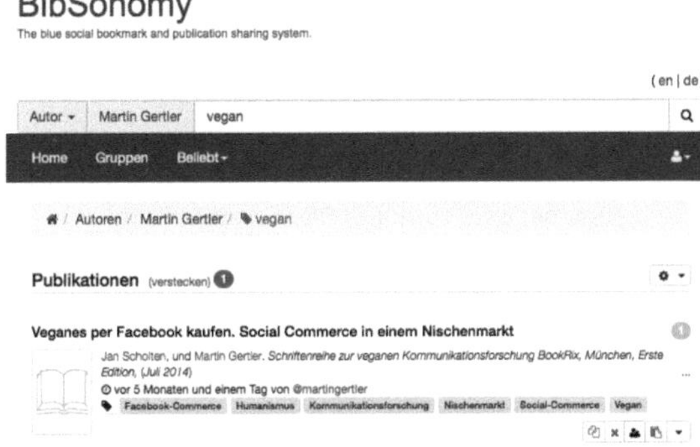

Figure 11: Search in BibSonomy

(Source: Screenshot of BibSonomy 2014d)

The output format must be selected accordingly. All formats are described in detail by Bibsonomy; basically, you only have to look for yourself which formats can be „understood" by your literature management program for importing.

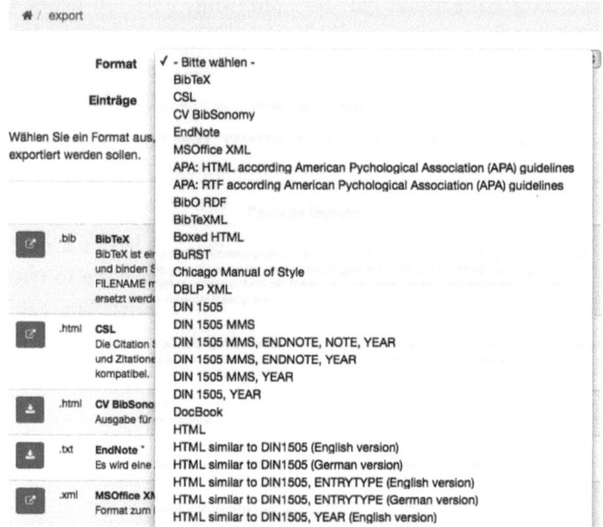

Figure 12: Select Format in BibSonomy

(Source: Screenshot of BibSonomy 2014a)

For manual processing in the electronic „card index", you can simply display the search result as an HTML page:

Jan Scholten, und Martin Gertler. **Veganes per Facebook kaufen. Social Commerce in einem Nischenmarkt.** In Martin Gertler (Hrsg.), Schriftenreihe zur veganen Kommunikationsforschung, (1)BookRix, München, Juli 2014. [BibSonomy: Facebook-Commerce Humanismus Kommunikationsforschung Nischenmarkt Social-Commerce Vegan Veganismus myown] URL

Figure 13: HTML Output of a Source in BibSonomy

(Source: Screenshot of BibSonomy 2014b)

The information contained in this HTML output format is required for entry in the electronic „card index", in this case: author, book title, series with publisher, volume, publisher's name, place of publication.

If you set up a free account with BibSonomy – operated by the FG Wissensverarbeitung of the University of Kassel, the DMIR Group of the University of Würzburg and the L3S Research Centre – you can also create your own publications there, which may not yet be included, so that they can be called up online faster than the usual way and their master data can be used by everyone.

For the browsers Chrome and Firefox, BibSonomy provides own add-ons to make the work easier for logged in users.

Figure 14: Browser Addons of BibSonomy

(Source: Screenshot of BibSonomy 2014c)

With these addons you can call up your own data management, set bookmarks and transfer a publication displayed in the browser to BibSonomy.

BibSonomy is therefore a practical aid when searching for literature data to be listed in your own bibliography – and it is also helpful to make your own publications available to all those who might be able to use them from the day of publication.

The output formats provided by BibSonomy not only cover our legendary „electronic card index", but can also be used for the import requirements of a literature management program, and can even output publication lists that can be integrated into websites, such as the complete publication list of the author of this book.

6.3   University Data

It is always worth taking a look at the holdings of universities, because they often have works in their data collections or can link to libraries linked to them that cannot be found in BibSonomy or elsewhere.

However, it can also happen the other way round – if you enter „Martin Gertler vegan" in your search at the University Library of Cologne, for example, you will not find the e-book as it was the case with BibSonomy:

Figure 15: Negative Search Result at Cologne University Library

(Source: Screenshot of the search result at the University of Cologne 2014b)

If, on the other hand, you are looking for data from a print edition, there is a good chance that you will find it directly in such university libraries:

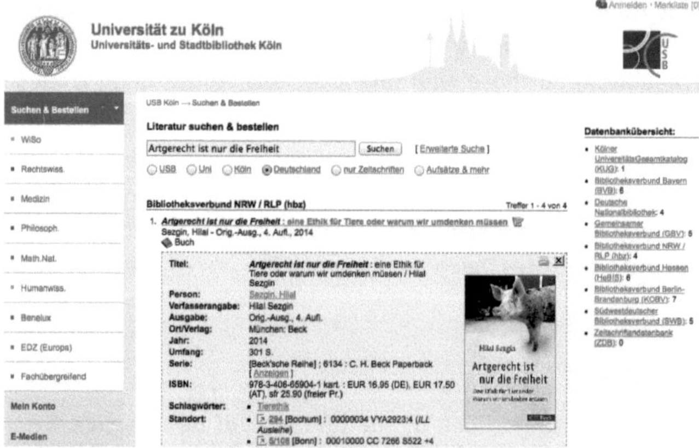

Figure 16: Positive Search Result at Cologne University Library

(Source: Screenshot of the search result of Uni Köln 2014c)

In this case, the title page of the book is also displayed here, so that you can quickly check whether the correct record for the book on your table has been found.

Using the small icon that leads to the „Bookmark List", this personal bookmark list can now be supplemented with the data of this book and then called up:

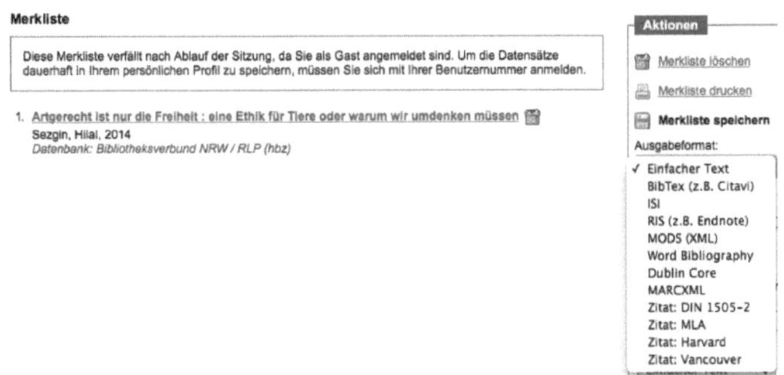

Figure 17: Wish List at Cologne University Library

(Source: Screenshot of the watch list of the University of Cologne 2014a)

The export formats are less variable here than with BibSonomy; for most transfer purposes in literature administration programs, however, the required data forms might be offered.

In any case, it is clear that data from print works can be found here in particular. You will also notice that special features are sometimes kept in linked external libraries, so that the literature data of rare copies can possibly be offered at least from there.

At this point, it should be noted that if you are looking for a book in this way that you do not yet have on your table, the interlibrary loan system can help you. Your university library can tell you how this works and what it can do for you.

6.4   Worldwide Data

As the third and last step to the data of your literature, OCLC WorldCat, the world's largest library catalog with online access to all library holdings, is presented to you.

This raises the question of whether the e-book by Jan Scholten and Martin Gertler can possibly be found here:

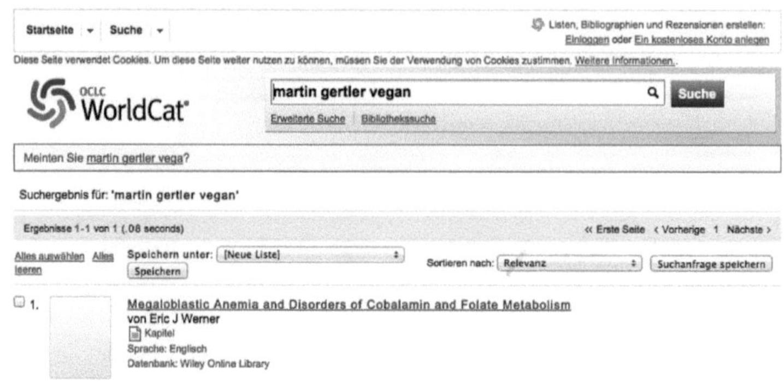

Figure 18: Negative Search Result for WorldCat

(Source: OCLC WorldCat 2014c search results screenshot)

So the book you are looking for cannot be found here either, instead you are referred to a database article that does not reflect the intended search result. The displayed result can be based on the fact that the searched words appear in the text of the referenced chapter.

In contrast to the University Library of Cologne, WorldCat does not display all individual occurrences in the search for „species-appropriate freedom alone" among each other, but groups them in folders.

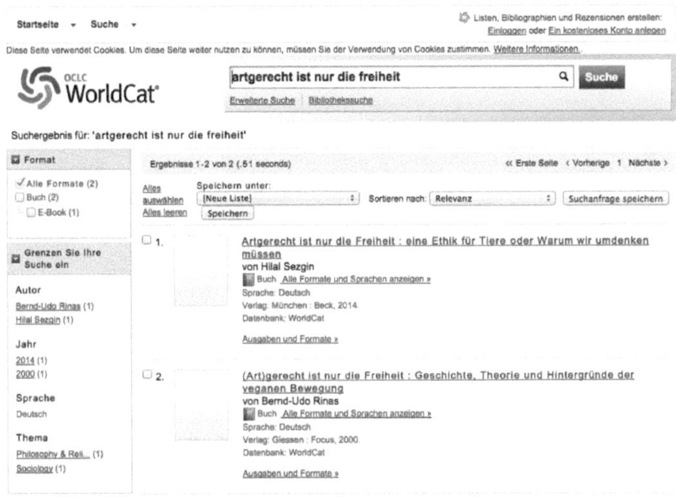

Figure 19: Overview of Found Works at WorldCat

(Source: Screenshot of OCLC WorldCat 2014a results overview)

In this case two folders became visible and one shows thereby fast that there was many years ago a book similar name and which is now the work looked for.

With the next screenshot the URL is also visible, so that you can discover that there is a small symbol at the end. By clicking, it imports the data of this book directly into your literature management program Zotero, if installed (see Roy Rosenzweig Center for History and New Media 2014).

Figure 20: Individual Book Data in WorldCat

(Source: Screenshot of a single OCLC WorldCat 2014b reference)

Worldcat is a useful, easy-to-use tool for everyday use, but it only knows works purchased from the cooperating libraries.

Our case study of a free e-book shows that it is good and useful to search for clues from BibSonomy and from other service providers at the same time.

6.5   Reference Manager

Now that we know that there are, so to speak, electronic index cards in which the metadata of quotable sources are stored, the question arises as to how they can be used most easily for one's own scientific work. The answer is clear: this is best done with a literature management program, also known as a reference manager.

The software helps us to keep track of the literature we are looking at for our work, to manage our own literature holdings and to keep them up to date. Above all, however, it helps to generate error-free and consistent source data.

Characteristic for literature management programs are the contained databases in which the metadata of sources are stored: Author, publisher, title of the work or contribution, date of publication, circulation, page range, URL, publisher's name and location, to name just a few of the most important data.

These data can usually be imported directly by such programs: through import functions, or even directly from standard web browsers.

If, for example, you have a book on your desk, you don't have to manually search and type in the metadata from the information it contains, but import it from the respective websites at Amazon, Bibsonomy, WorldCat or others.

The original texts themselves are not stored, because they are those monographs, collected works, journal articles, websites and other documents that we encountered during our research and from whose contents we need arguments and information for our own research.

A literature management program can output the source data used in your work as a source list in the usual citation styles, i.e. DIN 1505-2, MLA, APA and Harvard.

Universities and publishers always specify which citation style must be used to format the source lists of the studies to be submitted. Therefore, working with a literature management program is a good help: If, for example, you want to prepare a paper submitted to the university, which still had to be created with footnote references, and bring it to a publisher for publication, a mouse click is sometimes enough to switch from footnotes to In-Text references – provided that you had already created the original footnotes with the literature management program rather than manually.

Such literature management programs as Zotero, Citavi or EndNote work together with word processing programs. They make sure that for each citation in the text of the work there is a corresponding bibliographical information in the bibliography. They also ensure that, when the text is revised, removed source references lead to the corresponding cleansing of the source directory.

Web-based literature management programs also offer the possibility of collaborative cataloguing. For example, it is possible to generate mutual releases of data stocks for project or research groups. In this way, participants can achieve consistent source references in their joint research documentations.

One such web-based literature management program is Zotero. It is offered free of charge for all common operating systems and browsers.

With its help all references and the source list of this book were created.

6.6   Data Maintenance

The metadata of sources can always be entered manually in the Zotero literature management program.

To do this, create a new dataset, select the type of source to be entered and enter all the data required for this source.

Figure 21: Creating a Data Set in Zotero

Source: Own generation on 3 April 2015

It is easier to import directly from the browser – for example when visiting an online shop for books or an online catalogue of publications.

The small blue book icon at the top of the browser's URL line tells you that the Zotero browser plug-in is installed here and that the metadata of the book can be transferred to the Zotero database with a single click.

Below is a screenshot of the OCLC WorldCat retrieval, followed by a screenshot of the Amazon retrieval, each with the resulting Zotero database.

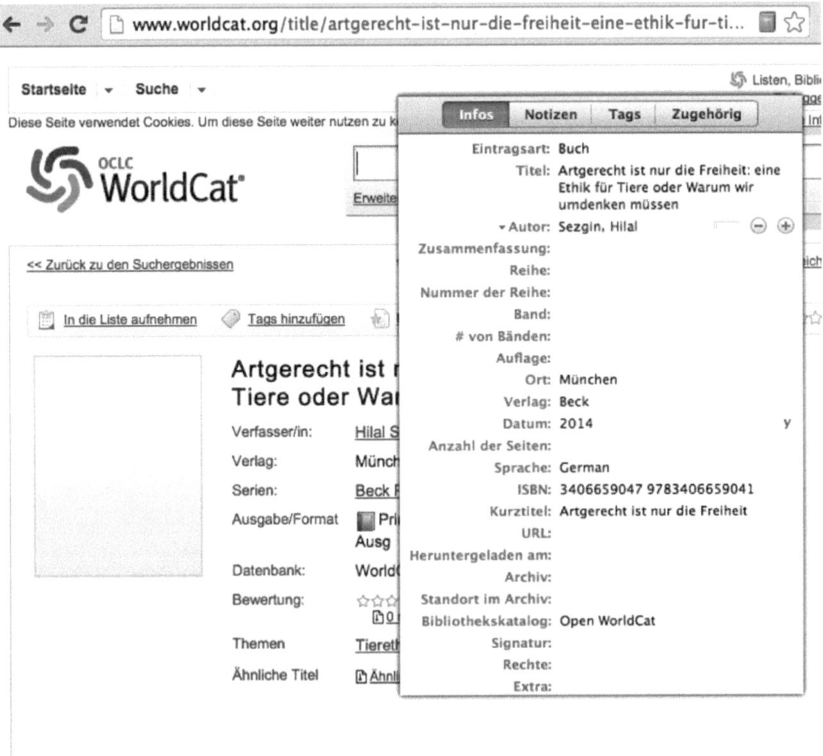

Figure 22: OCLC WorldCat Data Transfer

Source: Own generation on 3 April 2015

Figure 23: Data Transfer from Amazon

Source: Own generation on 3 April 2015

The comparison of the two images above as well as a quick test, i.e. the output of the data in an empty Word file, show which different data are available and that this results in different results:

(Sezgin 2014a) In-Text-Referenzierung mit Nutzung der OCLC-Daten

(Sezgin 2014b) In-Text-Referenzierung mit Nutzung der Amazon-Daten

Quellenverzeichnis:

Sezgin, Hilal (2014a): *Artgerecht ist nur die Freiheit: eine Ethik für Tiere oder Warum wir umdenken müssen*. München: Beck.

Sezgin, Hilal (2014b): *Artgerecht ist nur die Freiheit: Eine Ethik für Tiere oder Warum wir umdenken müssen*. 4. Aufl. München: C.H.Beck.

Figure 24: WorldCat / Amazon Results

Source: Own generation on 3 April 2015

The fact that the WorldCat data did not include a print run (second edition e.. a.) need not be an error: the library involved presumably contributed the data for the first print run – and a first print run is usually not specified.

Always look at the book you have on your table, from which you quote, and enter the corresponding edition into your Zotero database, because it could well be that the 4th edition contains additions and changes compared to an earlier edition – that is why edition details must be given precisely.

It is therefore important to make sure that the required information is actually available. It is also important to make sure that the vowel mutations and special characters contained are stored in such a way that they are reproduced correctly in the reference to the source. For example, if the university library entering WorldCat accidentally entered incorrect information for a source, or if correct-looking umlauts are initially incorrectly output in the work itself, for example „u¨ber" is then output instead of „über" in the source directory.

It is therefore recommended to critically check the respective data record immediately after each input and transfer into the Zotero database.

Direct import is also possible when visiting a website that is to be referenced as a source. However, in most cases some information has to be completed manually:

Figure 25: Transferring Data from an Online Source

Source: Own generation on 3 April 2015

Here the first and last name of the author and the year of the post had to be added.

Corrections are best made immediately and only in the database itself! If you correct the source information displayed in the actual text file of the work, it will be reset to the previous, incorrect state after the next refresh, because each entry of another source reference always leads to a refresh of all used data of your own Zotero database, so every error must always be corrected where it is stored: in the database.

6.7   Task Sheet for this Chapter

Support your self-study through these tasks!

1. Try out whether you can collect the metadata of your sources validly and completely according to the card index principle in MS Word – and whether the use of a reference manager (literature management program) would make more sense instead.

2. Check out the presented providers of metadata: BibSonomy, the offerings of your university library and WorldCat.org.

3. Try out the literature management programs presented – your university or publisher may have specific guidelines, and if not: Zotero should be the first choice, as it is available for all leading operating systems and is non-commercial.

4. Perform all necessary steps: manual input of metadata; adoption of metadata from online offers; preparation and correction of metadata; selection and change of output style.

7 Scientific Writing

Students who complete their studies must themselves prove good scientific practice. The DFG-Recommendations of the Commission *„Self-Regulation in Science: Proposals to Ensure Good Scientific Practice"* of January 1998 set out the criteria for this:

- to work according to recognized research standards of their own discipline,
- to document the results,
- to consistently doubt one's own results,
- to maintain honesty with regard to the contributions of third parties. (Cf. Deutsche Forschungsgemeinschaft 1998: 3 f.)

A violation of basic scientific rules is considered to be fraud. Such violations are fictitious or falsified data and plagiarisms.

Therefore, great care is required when writing – and constant assurance as to whether one meets these criteria of the German Research Foundation.

In this part, in the lesson on scientific writing, we address the question of how best to approach the necessary components of our work.

Structure of a Scientific Work

This can be done for *smaller* scientific assignments:

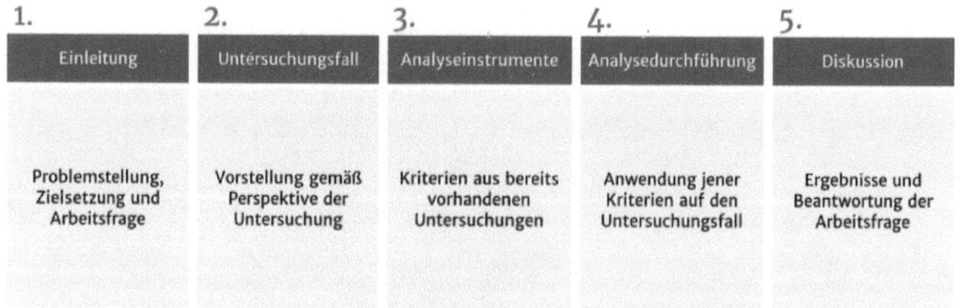

Figure 26: Structural Model of Smaller Works

Source: Own representation

After (1. Introduction) description and justification of the problem, a resulting objective for the investigation as well as the operationalizing research question is followed in the next chapter (2. Examination case) by the subject of the investigation, strictly from the perspective of the objective of the investigation.

Thereafter (3. Analytical tools) criteria from existing studies and, if necessary, additionally from professional sources are compiled and compiled into an analysis toolkit.

During the analysis (4. Analysis) they serve to test the object of analysis. The individual results of the analysis – whether arguing or based on measurement results – should also be recorded in tabular form together with their respective strengths.

In the last chapter (5. Discussion) there are no new aspects or contents – here the results together with their strength descriptions are interpreted with regard to the goal of the study and the working question is explicitly answered.

This can be done for *more extensive* scientific work:

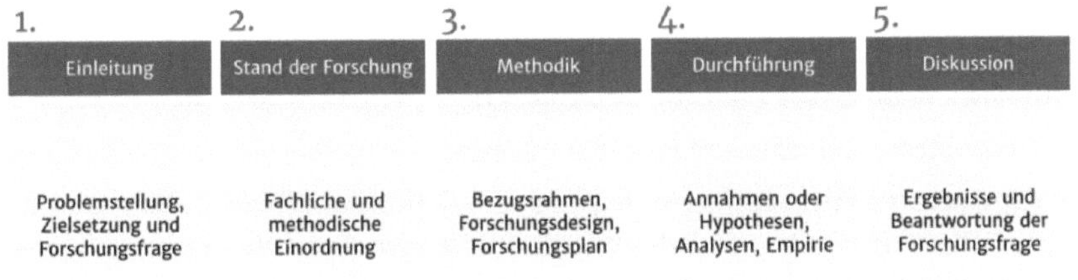

Figure 27: Structural Model of Larger Projects

Source: Own representation

After (1. Introduction) description and justification of the problem, a resulting objective for the investigation as well as the research question operationalizing it.

The following will describe in detail the state of research in the next step (2. Current state of research), strictly from the perspective of the objective of the study.

Then (3. Methodology) the frame of reference for the previous is defined and the research design is determined, including the well-founded choice of methods as well as the presentation of the chosen ways of using and implementing the methods.

In the next step (4. Implementation), assumptions or hypotheses are developed and examined by analysis or application of empirical methods, and the results obtained should also be recorded in tabular form together with their respective strengths.

In the last step (5. Discussion) there are no new aspects or contents – here the results together with their descriptions are interpreted with regard to the research objective and the research question is explicitly answered.

Steps 2 to 4 can extend over several chapters.

7.1 The Introduction

What belongs in your „introduction"? Neither thanksgiving nor personal reports belong in the first chapter of a scientific paper.

Readers rightly expect to be informed about the defined problem in a concise and comprehensible manner, to get to know the objective you set and to learn the research question you formulated for this purpose.

It is best to headline this first chapter with what appears in it – as well as all other headings always indicate the subject in the respective chapter:

    1 Problem, objective and research question

In the context of the first point, the problem definition, the delimitation of the topic is then also to be carried out and justified, whereby the consequences of the delimitation for the scope and generalization of the results and conclusions are to be explained there (cf. Franck 2009: 144)..

It is therefore better not to use the meaningless word „Introduction" as the chapter heading, but to clearly indicate in the heading what readers can expect in this first chapter: „Problem, objective and research question".

But don't let yourself be tempted to describe the three terms in sub-items, because then you have probably already become too detailed. The problem, objective and research question of a term paper, project or thesis should normally be presented together on a single page, in logical order.

7.2 Investigate independently

To achieve this, you have to formulate a claim which you have to meet at least when writing your thesis. In order to train for it, it is necessary to keep this standard also with housework. „Investigation" is an indication of the not only formal, but actually scientific character of the work. Consequently, this cannot be an essay or a purely practical problem-solving treatise.

Investigations are in principle *open-ended*, which makes them independent: their results are not predetermined. And this distinguishes them from practical tasks that were previously defined by the client – such as the development of a business model, a business plan or a communication measure.

Science knows only how to „find" solutions by following a methodical path, but not how to justify previously defined solutions and solution paths. Science can only find solutions by measuring or testing different possibilities against criteria that have been worked out.

In order to realize this, you need a research question at the beginning, which has to be answered in the last chapter on the basis of the processing part.

Thus, the task of a thesis differs from a „conception" in everyday professional life: In a course of study – certainly practice-oriented – it is primarily scientific to proceed and argue.

7.3   Integrating the Basics

In principle, nothing that is superfluous for the processing and answering of the research question or topic may occur in a scientific work. Positively formulated: Everything that is necessary for understanding the problem and the solution must be included in the work.

Of course, this includes basics from the scientific literature: methods, models and investigations that can already be found for the object of investigation. Nevertheless: please do not create a separate basic part (as a chapter 2)! Such a separate basic part often has to be filled with all sorts of information, which may not be needed at all in the actual processing that follows from chapter 3 onwards or which may have to be referred back to in each case - this results in a cumbersome leafing around for the reader.

Tip: Start your editing part directly with chapter 2 and always bring in basic information directly where it is necessary for argumentation or for traceability! In this way, you avoid the unnecessary preparation and writing of unnecessary information, you save time and energy – and your scientific work becomes more consistent.

The reason for this approach is to maintain the research character – the achievement of a knowledge goal – in all university work, including project work and presentations.

If you decide to create a chapter „State of Research" for your presumably more extensive project, make sure that there are only sources that will contribute comprehensibly to the problem, objective and solution finding.

7.4   The Final Chapter

Basically, no more new information belongs in your last chapter! So references to external sources are also out of place. Also unsuitable are considerations about the context of the topic, essay-like oracles about the significance of the work results for the future, or similar.

Please do not write a „final consideration" at all! This word does not indicate that your scientific final spurt is taking place here.

The conclusion of a thesis serves only to draw well-founded and comprehensible conclusions from the work previously done and to discuss them - no more and no less. Here is to place the research question formulated at the beginning again and to answer it explicitly, looking back and referring to the previous chapters.

Should it say: „Conclusion and outlook"? To overwrite the final chapter with „Conclusion and Outlook" seems a little better. Thus it becomes apparent that the results of the research question can be found here and that conclusions are presented.

However, it must be strictly ensured that these „outlooks" are actually drawn logically from the results of the previous chapters, but are not simply written down as allegations!

Best: „Discussion of the results"!

This heading for the concluding chapter is usually the best one, because it lets you expect to repeat the research question here, to give an answer to the research question from summaries of the results obtained and to discuss all this critically – including your approach and methodology.

In addition, „Discussion of the results" is an optimal heading for your final chapter because, as is well known, it cannot consist of making assertions, but only of making comprehensible arguments.

Whether interim or final conclusion: there are no more references to external sources, at most to your own (sub)chapters! A conclusion should not bring something new, otherwise it would not be a conclusion. So the focus will only be on your own conclusions, which you had drawn before, but not on the leading positions of others.

If anyone wants to read the data and arguments that led to those conclusions, he has to look up where they were presented and discussed.

7.5   Cost-effective Data Evaluation

In some cases Excel may be sufficient, but not for statistical scientific work as a rule. However, you can use the open source software PSPP (free of charge), because SPSS is expensive software.

If possible, do it this way:

- Install PSPP, enter your own data there, perform the required calculations and have the results output to you.

- You can then take the SPSS-compatible file with you on a stick to university and have SPSS calculate the results there.

- You output the results there as a PDF, copy them to the stick and can transfer them to the (creationor appendix of your) work.

The background to this detour via an existing SPSS installation is that PSPP is open source software and therefore it cannot always be guaranteed that statistically exact calculations will actually be output.

7.6   General Rules of Citation

Quotations must always be recognizable, and they must be translated exactly in form and correctly in content.

If the original quotation has spelling and punctuation that deviate from our current rules, these deviations must also be adopted, provided it is a literal, direct quotation. With analogous, indirect quotations such deviations are not taken over, because we reproduce the foreign content with our own words.

Literal, direct quotations can be recognized by the fact that the foreign text is placed in quotation marks. Non-literal, meaningful or indirect quotations are the norm in everyday scientific life; they do not appear in quotation marks.

Before the foreign text begins, it must become clear that someone else is now „speaking“ – and the short reference must follow the foreign text.

7.7   Tables of Figures

There are different directories for figures and tables, which can be set up using the normal functions of Word or OpenOffice.

Insert illustrations or tables into the document and right-click on the activated element to select: „Insert caption...“.

Now enter a brief, comprehensible description there, just as you would for headlines – example: „Sales development 2004 to 2014“.

This title then appears automatically in the corresponding directory (for figures or tables), maintaining automatic numbering („Figure 3“ or „Table 3“).

7.8   Types of Sources in the Bibliography

Even a literature management program like Zotero can only output the literature data stored in its database in the way we have marked it, so it is helpful to take a closer look at the different occurrences.

The examples given in the bibliography correspond to the standard output using Zotero in Harvard style.

Monographs

Surname, first name of author (year): title (= series if applicable), edition (from 2.), place of publication

> Sezgin, Hilal (2014): *Artgerecht ist nur die Freiheit. Eine Ethik für Tiere oder Warum wir umdenken müssen.* Munich: Verlag C.H. Beck.

Contributions in Anthologies

Name, first name of author, (year): title, in: name, first name of publisher (ed.): title of anthology, place of publication, page numbers from to

> Riesenhuber, Felix (2009): „Großzahlige empirische Forschung“ In: Albers, Sönke (ed.) *Methodik der empirischen Forschung.* Wiesbaden: Deutscher Universitäts-Verlag pp. 1-16.

Articles in journals

Name, first name of author (year): title, in: name of journal, volume, number of pages

Gertler, Martin (2013): »Meaning-generating propositions of reality by media: Quality attributes and functions of journalism«. In: *Journal of Information, Communication and Ethics in Society*. 11 (1), S. 4–18.

Contributions from the Internet

Name, first name of author, (year if possible): Title, complete URL (status, retrieval date)

Hagen, Tobias (2014): „Evidenzbasierte Wirtschaftspolitik: CO2-Bilanz von Lebensmitteln", retrieved on 19.01.2015 from http://evidenzbasierte-wirtschaftspolitik.blogspot.de/2014/12/co2-bilanz-von-lebensmitteln.html.

If PDF, please save an electronic copy of the quoted original text and submit it if necessary.

7.9　Required Elements

An *abstract* is expected for most forms of publication; this is not the case for university theses.

In any case, the *table of contents* must begin by showing the structure in a staged and clear form, with the usual numbering and the respective page numbers. The table of contents is generated automatically by the word processing program itself, as long as you have worked with the corresponding format assignments for each heading. Handmade tables of contents should be avoided – experience has shown them to be a source of errors: suddenly the page numbers are incorrect and sometimes the chapter headings in the paper are different from those in the directory.

The chapters with ordinal numbers begin with the *introduction* and end with the *final chapter*. All elements outside have no numbering.

Appendices can be structured as „Appendix A", „Appendix B" etc., with subitems „A.1", „A.2", etc.

Any annexes are followed by the *optional glossary*, in which terms requiring explanation are described in an understandable manner.

Then follow the *list of figures* and *the list of tables* – both are only necessary if at least one figure or at least one table is present in the paper (including in the appendix).

If abbreviations not generally known have been used, they will be included in the otherwise *optional list of abbreviations* and will be reproduced there in alphabetical order in full.

Afterwards, the necessary *declaration of independence* signed must be inserted, followed by a *curriculum vitae* and, if applicable, an *index*. Without the declaration, a thesis will not be accepted or cannot be considered as passed.

7.10 University Standards

Some habits of daily language and writing have no place in a scientific work, i.e. an investigation that is about precision and conciseness.

The problems begin as soon as the terms of the examination regulations and the prescribed examination forms are abandoned in favour of one's own word creations.

For example, a „booklet" is not one of the scientific products (such as homework, seminar papers, bachelor thesis, master thesis and dissertation), but is defined in linguistic usage rather as a by-product of CD and DVD packaging (cf. Wikipedia 2014). „Booklets" describe the resume of an artist who presents his work on the CD or DVD, or they have been created for the electronic part of the offer in training media.

The specifications for the above-mentioned scientific products (also called „scientific artifacts") can be found in the standard works valid at many universities (cf. Balzert et al. 2011; cf. also Rossig and Prätsch 2008). These are university guidelines.

The qualification goals of higher education degree programmes require that all modules have a scientific basis. In principle, there are no non-scientific subjects/modules at (applied) scientific universities. The forms of examination must be designed accordingly: Scientific qualifications must always be examined in addition to practical professional qualifications. The mere creation of occupation-oriented products as well as the description (recording) of their occurrence is not sufficient as an examination performance.

This of course also has an impact on the form of the submissions: they alone must meet scientific standards and must therefore not „formatively" deviate from scientific requirements. Where this is nevertheless recommended or demanded in individual cases by non-scientifically profiled reviewers, one should withdraw to the scientifically oriented guidelines for scientific work (written e.g. in the form of a general guideline of the university) and work unchanged with the centrally provided templates.

7.11   No „Dork Blanks"

This well-known, deliberately unfriendly term, which has been coined by a blog of the same name (cf. Guest 2004), serves to identify an increasingly frequent error in German writing – not only in scientific papers, but above all in the marketing language.

For example, cans are labeled with such stuttering: „Tomaten Stücke" (tomato pieces, „Kirchererbsen Eintopf" (chickpea stew) and „Kidney Bohnen" (kidney beans), whereas in German language the only correct labels for the three cans mentioned would be the following: „Zomatenstücke" (or, to maintain the two lines on the label: „Tomaten-Stücke"), „Kirchererbsen-Eintopf" and „Kidneybohnen".

This misspelling is increasingly spilling over from professional life into scientific papers. Above all, many mistakenly believe that all compound words are not written together in English and that this is consequently (?) not the case in German either.

But you can also find in the English summaries – „Firstclass passengers" are at least as common and more clearly described as the equally common „first class passengers". Separate and concise descriptions always determine meaning and comprehensibility!

According to Duden, however, German spelling always dominates the procedure for composing with English terms: „First-class-Passagiere", „Content-Management-Systeme", „Public-Relations-Abteilung". Here the Duden is clear: *„In the case of sequences and compositions with word groups, the word must always be hyphenated"* (Duden 2013c).

According to Duden, even the complete adoption of English terms consisting of several nouns does not protect against the obligation of composition: shop signs with information such as „Coffee Bar" and „Hair Stylist" are wrong in German, so adoption of terms such as „Marketing Management" or „Content Management" into German necessarily leads to the compilation: „Marketingmanagement", „Contentmanagement" etc. For long compositions, hyphens can also be used: „Desktop-Publishing" (cf. Duden 2013d).

However, if the first part of the composition is not a noun but an adjective (e.g. „black box") and the main emphasis is on the first part, you have the option of writing it separately; however, the Duden recommends that you also write it together in this case.

In separate spelling, it remains based on English if a combination of adjective and noun is written separately and no emphasis is placed on the first part („electronic banking", „top ten", etc.). (Cf. Duden 2013c)

Who wants to avoid not only a worse grading, but also the ugly stamp of the lecturer „dork blanks" next to the texts in his work, takes as far as possible distance from any „dork blanks".

7.12   Consistent Page Numbers

Do you still need to use roman page numbers? No, because in times of the usual submission of PDF versions of homework and final papers, a different page count (first Roman, then Arabic after the introduction, and finally Roman again) only causes confusion.

If your reviewer reads in the table of contents of the PDF that chapter 3 starts for example on page 7, then he must be able to easily enter the page number „7" in the Acrobat-Reader to get there without ending up on page 3 or similar instead.

Because of different counting methods within a document, the validity of the information in the table of contents would be lost, which is why most universities now refrain from demanding this outdated presentation method (since it is based on mere paper submissions) as a standard.

In times of PDF files, online journals and e-books, such peculiarities, which are certainly traditional but have always been difficult to implement, can no longer be maintained.

7.13   Evaluation and Grading

Basically, the evaluation of a scientific work will be based on the specifications, which in turn refer to different criteria.

First of all, of course, the basic requirements of the respective examination regulations must be observed, based on the information on the final thesis, to which all previous scientific work must already be directed.

These requirements are usually formulated in this way or similarly in the applicable examination regulations:

In short:

- prescribed time
- practical topic from the field of study
- incorporating current scientific findings
- an independent investigation.

This already makes it clear that there is no room for „essays" here, but that an *investigation* is expected.

Accordingly, appropriate evaluation criteria are applied and weighted to a different extent during the audit; they are formulated in this or similar ways:

1. topic and research question, hypotheses
2. structuring
3. conceptual–theoretical basics
4. effectuation
5. sources and citation
6. shape and style

The examiners pay attention to special characteristics per criterion, e.g. like this:

1. Topic and research question, hypotheses: The topic is topical and relevant for science and practice; it is challenging; the problem is clearly and unambiguously defined; relevant research gaps are identified; the objectives are presented; research questions and hypotheses are clearly formulated and justified; methods and concepts are independent of a company or a specific problem.

2. Structuring: The structure is formally correct, logically formulated and meaningful; it has a depth appropriate to the subject matter; the structuring of the argument follows a scientific method (deduction, induction, comparative method); the subdivision is practical, complete and con-

sistent; the structuring points are formulated in a substantiated form; a „common thread" is clearly visible.

3. Conceptual-theoretical foundations: A conceptual-theoretical part is available; definitions of central terms and an appropriate delimitation of terms are available; a description of the fundamentals and research statuses required for the investigation is available; the choice of theory is justified in terms of content; the essential subject aspects are taken into account, a reduction to certain partial aspects is justified; the work identifies gaps in the status of research that are to be closed during the course of the study.

4. Implementation: A concrete practical problem is identified, analysed and described in a structured manner; the scientific methods researched are applied to the object under investigation; a solution is developed for the problem by means of a suitable, systematic and structured procedure; problem analysis, method selection and application and development of the solution approach are carried out correctly and independently; the developed approach is suitable and realisable for solving the problem in hand; the procedure and problem solution are documented in a structured form in writing and comprehensibly for the expert reader; illustrations, diagrams, graphics and diagrams are available in sufficient quality.

5. Sources and citation method: adequate scientific sources (monographs, scientific journals, working papers etc.) are taken into account to an appropriate extent; the use of empirical studies is available; the selection of sources corresponds to the current state of research; all sources are worthy of citation (primary sources, topicality, trustworthiness etc.); practical information (e.g. company and industry specifics) is taken into account if additionally necessary; a critical distance is recognizable when evaluating the sources; the exact identification of all external sources is ensured by correct, consistent citation technique; the citation is possible.

6. Form and style: the expressions are clear and precise, no colloquial formulations are used; language efficiency is given (no repetitions); clear thought guidance (1 thought = 1 paragraph) is recognizable; appropriate use of foreign words and relevant technical terms is given; correct use of the rules of spelling, grammar and punctuation is given; a correct external form (cover page, declaration of independence, curriculum vitae) is present; the tables and illustrations are easy to read; the required directories (table of contents, list of sources, if necessary image)

It is important to be in tune with such criteria and their characteristics from the outset: during the general inspection of a motorized vehicle, a checklist of characteristics is also processed – admittedly, such measurement data are less subject to personal assessment than the criteria and characteristics for the evaluation of scientific work, but it is helpful to keep in mind when preparing and writing the work: one's own enthusiasm – which inevitably arises once there are only ten, twenty pages full – is not sufficient as an assessment yard-stick, but there are just those other standards.

It is best to ask your examiners in advance and early enough what standards they will apply – it is right to know where you will be measured!

You really have to be guided by the standards for assessing a degree dissertation from the very beginning, right from the very first term paper to be submitted. It is important to take the guidelines and requirements of the supervisors very seriously so that you get closer to your goal as quickly as possible.

7.14 Supplementary Remark

It's like learning to swim: just wading a little through the shallow water on the beach doesn't help you discover and develop your swimming skills. If you don't take the swimming instructor's advice seriously, you'll either never experience the fascination of swimming or even run the risk of going under if you suddenly and unexpectedly have to rely on your swimming skills.

Studying is similar: without training in scientific work, you don't discover it and end up stranded, you don't achieve your goal, namely the completion of a university degree.

If the hurdle of getting involved in clean scientific work is too high for someone because he doesn't like it or doesn't succeed (usually both are connected: what you don't like, you don't succeed either): then you should rather break it off early and look for other challenges that fit your own life plan.

To find out if you really don't like it, you should have tried it at least once with care and with great seriousness!

7.15   Task Sheet for this Chapter

Support your self-study through these tasks!

1. Outline how you would structure your research project yourself – and compare it with the two models offered in this lesson. Then edit your concept.

2. In order to conduct research openly, a corresponding description of the project and the corresponding choice of language (expression) during writing are necessary. Design your own guidelines for the implementation.

3. As soon as you make progress with your examination and results are achieved, write them down in a separate file each time, so that they are available all the faster and nothing can be left out accidentally.

4. Familiarize yourself with the evaluation and grading standards of your university and apply them immediately to even the smallest scientific work in order to train early for the final track.

List of Figures

Bibliography

Balzert, Helmut; Schröder, Marion; Schäfer, Christian (2011): *Wissenschaftliches Arbeiten – Ethik, Inhalt & Form wiss. Arbeiten, Handwzeug, Quellen, Projektmanagement, Präsentation.* 2nd edition. Herdecke; Witten: W3L-Verlag.

BibSonomy (2014a): „Bibsonomy: Ausgabeformate". http://www.bibsonomy.org/export/author/Martin%20Gertler/vegan?lang=en retrieved on 30/12/2014.

BibSonomy (2014b): „Bibsonomy: Ausgabe in HTML". Retrieved on 30.12.2014 from http://www.bibsonomy.org/publ/author/Martin%20Gertler/vegan?lang=en&items=100.

BibSonomy (2014c): „Bibsonomy: Browser-Addons". Retrieved on 30/12/2014 from http://www.bibsonomy.org/help_en/Google%20Chrome-%20or%20Mozilla%20Firefox-Addon%20.

BibSonomy (2014d): „Bibsonomy: Suchergebnis". Retrieved on 12/30/2014 from http://www.bibsonomy.org/author/Martin%20Gertler/vegan?lang=en.

Bortz, Jürgen; Döring, Nicola (2009): *Forschungsmethoden und Evaluation für Human- und Sozialwissenschaftler; mit 87 Tabellen.* Heidelberg: Springer-Medizin-Verlag.

Brink, Alfred (2005): *Anfertigung wissenschaftlicher Arbeiten: ein prozessorientierter Leitfaden zur Erstellung von Bachelor-, Master- und Diplomarbeiten in acht Lerneinheiten.* Munich, Vienna: Oldenbourg.

Bünting, Karl-Dieter; Bitterlich, Axel; Pospiech, Ulrike (2008): *Schreiben im Studium: mit Erfolg.* Berlin: Cornelsen Scriptor.

Deutsche Forschungsgemeinschaft (Ed.) (1998): *Sicherung guter wissenschaftlicher Praxis:* Weinheim: WILEY-VCH.

Duden (2013a): „Kriterium". Retrieved on 28.12.2014 from http://www.duden.de/rechtschreibung/Kriterium.

Duden (2013b): „Merkmal". Retrieved on 28.12.2014 from http://www.duden.de/rechtschreibung/Merkmal.

Duden (2013c): „Schreibung von Fremdwörtern aus dem Englischen". Retrieved on 11.01.2015 from
http://www.duden.de/sprachwissen/sprachratgeber/schreibung-von-fremdwoertern-aus-dem-englischen.

Duden (2013d): „Zusammengesetzte Substantive". Retrieved on 11.01.2015 from
http://www.duden.de/sprachwissen/sprachratgeber/zusammengesetzte-substantive.

Dürr, Hans-Peter (2011): *Warum es ums Ganze geht – Neues Denken für eine Welt im Umbruch.* Frankfurt/Main: Fischer-Taschenbuch-Verlag.

Von Foerster, Heinz (1997): *Einführung in den Konstruktivismus: Beiträge von Heinz von Foerster, Ernst von Glasersfeld, Peter M. Hejl, Siegfried J. Schmidt, Paul Watzlawick.* Munich: Piper.

Franck, Norbert (2009): *Die Technik wissenschaftlichen Arbeitens – Eine praktische Anleitung.* Paderborn; Munich; Vienna; Zurich: Schöningh.

Frank, Andrea.; Haacke, Stefanie.; Lahm, Swantje. (2007): *Schlüsselkompetenzen: Schreiben in Studium und Beruf.* Stuttgart; Weimar: Metzler.

Gast, Titus (2004): „Deppenleerzeichen | Alleinstellungsmerkmal". Retrieved on 11.01.2015 from http://deppenleerzeichen.de.

Gertler, Martin (1997a): „Aus Sternenstaub - Der Mensch im Kosmos". *Director's Cut.* Retrieved on 25.12.2014 from http://vimeo.com/15086035.

Gertler, Martin (1997b): „Hans-Peter Dürr: Das Geistige ist die treibende Kraft". Retrieved on December 25, 2014 from
http://youtu.be/lrgQakHPRP8.

Gertler, Martin (2013): „Online-Lehre? Am besten asynchron". Retrieved on 03.04.2015 from http://gertler.net/archives/2433.

Gertler, Martin (1999): *Unterwegs zu einer Fernsehgemeinde: Erfahrung von Kirche durch Gottesdienstübertragungen.* 2nd edition. Cologne: KIM.

Gertler, Martin (1997c): „Wirklichkeit und Wahrheit - Paul Watzlawick". Retrieved on 24.12.2014 from http://youtu.be/LEmZ2GOxzo8?t=1m39s.

Hagen, Tobias (2014): „Evidenzbasierte Wirtschaftspolitik: CO2-Bilanz von Lebensmitteln". Retrieved on 19.01.2015 from http://evidenzbasierte-wirtschaftspolitik.blogspot.de/2014/12/co2-bilanz-von-lebensmitteln.html.

Hennecke, Marcus; Moore, Ross; Swan, Herb (2001): „Variable (Merkmal)". Retrieved from http://eswf.uni-koeln.de/glossar/node10.html.

Jungert, Michael (Ed.) (2010): *Interdisciplinarität: Theorie, Praxis, Probleme* Darmstadt: Wissenschaftliche Buchgesellschaft.

Jung, Matthias (2012): *Hermeneutik zur Einführung*. Hamburg: Junius.

Karmasin, Matthias; Ribing, Rainer (2006): *Die Gestaltung wissenschaftlicher Arbeiten: ein Leitfaden für Haus- und Seminararbeiten, Magisterarbeiten, Diplomarbeiten und Dissertationen* Vienna: WUV.

KoraChany (2015): „Wann wird wissenschaftliches Arbeiten eingesetzt? (Wissenschaft)". *gutefrage.net*. Retrieved on 03.04.2015 from http://www.gutefrage.net/frage/wann-wird-wissenschaftliches-arbeiten-eingesetzt.

OCLC WorldCat (2014a): „Ergebnis für „artgerecht ist nur die freiheit"". Retrieved on 30/12/2014 from http://www.worldcat.org/search?q=artgerecht+ist+nur+die+freiheit&qt=results_page.

OCLC WorldCat (2014b): „Ergebnis für „Artgerecht ist nur die Freiheit – Eine Ethik für Tiere oder Warum wir umdenken müssen". Retrieved 30.12.2014 from http://www.worldcat.org/title/artgerecht-ist-nur-die-freiheit-eine-ethik-fur-tiere-oder-warum-wir-umdenken-mussen/oclc/869854207&referer=brief_results.

OCLC WorldCat (2014c): „Ergebnis für "martin gertler vegan"". Retrieved December 30, 2014 from http://www.worldcat.org/search?qt=worldcat_org_all&q=martin+gertler+vegan.

Popper, Karl R. (1966): *Logik der Forschung*. Tübingen: Mohr (Siebeck).

Pörksen, Bernhard (2002): *Die Gewissheit der Ungewissheit: Gespräche zum Konstruktivismus*. Heidelberg: Carl-Auer-Systems.

Riesenhuber, Felix (2009): „Großzahlige empirische Forschung". In: Albers, Sönke (ed.) *Methodik der empirischen Forschung*. Wiesbaden: Deutscher Universitäts-Verlag pp. 1-16.

Rossig, Wolfram E; Prätsch, Joachim (2008): *Wissenschaftliche Arbeiten: Leitfaden für Haus- und Seminararbeiten, Bachelor- und Masterthesis, Diplom- und Magisterarbeiten, Dissertationen.* Achim: BerlinDruck.

Roy Rosenzweig Center for History and New Media (2014): „Documentation". Retrieved on 14.02.2015 from http://zotero.org/support/quick_start_guide.

Sezgin, Hilal (2014): *Artgerecht ist nur die Freiheit. Eine Ethik für Tiere oder Warum wir umdenken müssen.* Munich: Verlag C.H. Beck.

Statista (2013): „Hilfe & FAQ". 11.01.2015. Retrieved from http://de.statista.com/statistik/tipps/.

Uni Köln(2014a): „USB :: Merkliste". Retrieved from http://goo.gl/P3RZJn. on 30.12.2014.

Uni Köln (2014b): „USB :: Suchen & Bestellen". Retrieved on 30.12.2014 from http://goo.gl/CAxST6.

Uni Köln (2014c): „:: Search & Order". Retrieved on 30.12.2014 from http://goo.gl/nb5lR8.

veganomics.de (2014): „Studie: Bereits 1,5 Prozent Veganer". *veganomics.de.* Retrieved on 09/06/2014 from http://veganomics.de/aktuelles/meldungen/20140312.php.

Weischenberg, Siegfried (1998): *Journalistik 1: Mediensysteme, Medienethik, Medieninstitutionen* Opladen: Westdeutscher Verlag.

Wikipedia (2014): „CD- und DVD-Verpackungen". *wikipedia.* Retrieved on 11.01.2015 from http://de.wikipedia.org/w/index.php?title=CD_and_DVD packaging&oldid=136812768.

Wissenschaftsrat (Ed.) (2011): „Empfehlungen zur Bewertung und Steuerung von Forschungsleistung" Drs. 1656-11.

ZEIT ONLINE (2014): „Multiresistente Keime: Diese Keime töten". 20.11.2014. Retrieved on 18.06.2016 from http://www.zeit.de/wissen/gesundheit/2014-11/multiresistente-keime-mrsa-antibiotika-massentierhaltung-keimkarte

About the Learn2Research.net Initiative

The website serves as basic and free support for all those who are looking for basic and application knowledge for scientific work.

It is the result of the in Germany unique initiative launched in 2010 to create FAQs for scientific work online and to allow them to continue to grow.

In the meantime several online offers can be found bundled:

- **FAQ**, which are constantly updated and supplemented
- **Webinars** for citation, development of the research question, working with a literature management program and empirical research
- **Online courses** – both for the book „Learn to Research" and for working with the reference manager Zotero
- **News** from the practice of scientific work

With the help of this website, everyone can continue their education anonymously.

Except for webinar registration or coaching, no personal data is collected and the data from the quizzes of the interactive videos in the online courses are only displayed to the respective user at the time of creation and are no longer stored.

The website has been optimized for mobile use in accordance with current standards („mobile first").

http://learn2research.net

learn2research.net

About the Author

Martin Gertler received his doctorate in 1999 from the University of Nijmegen (Netherlands) with an interdisciplinary study on the reception of a TV series.

Since 2002 he is professor for media design (especially audio visual and interactive media), media production, media theories and reception research in the media department of the Rheinische Fachhochschule Köln, a university of applied sciences.

In 2008 he was appointed founding rector of a new research university for continuing education in Berlin and for university professor.

Since 2011 he is visiting professor for doctoral supervision and promotor in the part-time graduate college of the University of Humanistic Studies / Universiteit voor Humanistiek, Utrecht (Netherlands).

In 2011 he founded the Humanistic Communication Research Institute (HCRI) and in 2015 together with other colleagues the Veganomics Institute.

He produces his audio-visual teaching media with his own resources.

http://tele-vision.de

Publications

2018

- Learn to Research – Tips for Scientific Working *(Book and Online Course)*
- Forschen lernen – Tipps zum wissenschaftlichen Arbeiten *(Book, 2nd ed.)*
- How to Develop your Research Question – Examples from Webinars *(Book)*
- Empirisch forschen – Ergänzende Einführung in das sozialwissenschaftliche Arbeiten *(Online Course)*

2017

- Entwicklung einer Forschungsfrage – Handreichung mit Beispielen aus der Hochschulpraxis *(Book)*
- Die Forschungsfrage *(Webinar)*
- Empirisch forschen *(3 Webinars)*

2016

- Richtig zitieren – Plagiate vermeiden *(Webinar)*
- Forschen. Grundlagen und Tipps für wissenschaftliche Arbeiten *(Book)*
- Literaturverwaltung mit Zotero *(Online Course)*
- Referenzmanager Zotero *(Webinar)*
- Sprachreisen für Jugendliche – Analyse eines Konzepts *(with Kai Wienands, Book)*

2015

- Forschen lernen – Tipps zum wissenschaftlichen Arbeiten *(Online Course)*
- Zwei Paradigmen nebeneinander: Meinungsbildung durch klassische vs. Interaktive Medien. In: M. Friedrichsen und R. A. Kohn (Ed.): Digitale Politikvermittlung – Chancen und Risiken interaktiver Medien *(Article)*
- Forschen lernen – Tipps zum wissenschaftlichen Arbeiten *(Book, 1st ed.)*

2014

- Veganes per Social Media kaufen – Social Commerce in einem Nischenmarkt *(with Jan Scholten, Book)*
- Twitter und der öffentliche Diskurs – Medienethische Fragen zur Funktion des Microblogging-Dienstes *(with Matthias Weiler, Book)*
- Humanismus und Veganismus *(Working Paper)*

2013

- Meaning-generating Propositions of Reality by Media – Quality Attributes and Functions of Journalism. Journal of Information, Communication & Ethics in Society, 11(1) *(Article)*

- Online-Lehre? Am besten asynchrony *(Statement)*

2012

- Der Kult um die „Journals" *(Statement)*
- Partizipation und Mystagogie als Leistungsmerkmale der Regie – Grund-konzeption eines Fernsehformats *(Book)*

2011

- Medien zwischen Ökonomie und Qualität: Medienethik als Instrument der Medienwirtschaft *(with Mike Friedrichen, Book)*
- Promotionsverfahren brauchen mehr Sicherheit *(Statement)*
- Zwischen Ökonomie und Ethik – Zur Qualität in Theorie und Praxis des Journalismus *(Book)*

2010

- Fachhochschule wird immer mehr Uni *(Statement)*

2009

- Abwertung der niederländischen Hogescholen? *(Statement)*

2007

- Wieviel Wissenschaftlichkeit verträgt Design? In: M. Gertler et al. (Eds.): Kölner Akzente zum Mediendesign

2005

- Literatur-Rundschau: „Liturgie in beeld" *(Review)*

2004

- Für „User" produzieren – Eine rezipientenorientierte Konzeptionsmetho-dik, *and*
- Mehr als Flimmern und Rauschen – Grundlagen der Bewegtbild-Kommunikation, *in:*

- Kommunikation oder Unterhaltung? Aufgabenstellungen der Medien *(Ed., Book)*

2002

- Umsetzen statt Gestalten? TV-Formatismus und persönliche Kreativität. In: M. Krzeminski (Herausgeber): Professionalität der Kommunikation – Medienberufe zwischen Auftrag und Autonomie *(Article)*

2001

- Wenig Feierlichkeit auf dem Bildschirm – Gottesdienstübertragungen im deutschen Fernsehen. In: P. Post et al. (Eds.): Christian Feast and Festival: The Dynamics of Western Liturgy and Culture *(Article)*

1999

- Unterwegs zu einer Fernsehgemeinde. Erfahrung von Kirche durch Gottesdienstübertragungen *(Book, 2nd ed.)*

1981

- Richtungswechsel – Über einen Versuch, TV zu einem Kommunikationsmittel zu machen. In: L. Huth und M. Krzeminski (Eds.): Zuschauerpost - ein Folgeproblem massenmedialer Kommunikation *(Article)*